THE ART OF AFRICAN FASHION

Prince Claus Fund, THE NETHERLANDS
Africa World Press, ERITREA/USA
1998

THE ART OF AFRICAN FASHION

The Prince Claus Fund stimulates and supports activities in the field of culture and development by presenting annual awards, by funding and producing publications and by financing and promoting intercultural exchange. Equality, respect and trust are the essential parameters of partnerships; quality and innovation are the preconditions of support. The Fund was established to mark the 70th birthday of HRH Prince Claus of the Netherlands on 6 September 1996. It represents an appreciation of his lifelong efforts stressing the importance of culture in international co-operation and of his achievements in this field.

The Fund adopts a broad and dynamic approach to culture, based on the concept of constant change. Culture is those values and processes which invest life with meaning through professional artistic achievements and academic work in the humanities. The Fund's chief interest is in the development of ideas and ideals, the manner in which people give form to these ideas and ideals and the manner in which such ideas and ideals give form to society.

This book has been published to mark the presentation of the Principal 1998 Prince Claus Award to The Art of African Fashion, honouring the arts of fashion design, textile design, hair design and body decoration – in short all arts relating to the decoration of human beings and the expression of the Self. The Prince Claus Fund acknowledges the artistic, social and economic importance of this industry in Africa and its influence on the international world of culture. The award was presented by HRH Prince Claus of the Netherlands on 9 December 1998 at the Royal Palace in Amsterdam. The laureates, representing The Art of African Fashion were Alphadi (Niger), Oumou Sy (Senegal) and Tetteh Adzedu (Ghana). The publication also accompanies the exhibition 'African Fashion Design' in the Stedelijk Museum in Amsterdam, held from 12 December 1998 until 31 January 1999.

The Art of African Fashion has been produced in co-operation with the Eritrean publisher Africa World Press in order to ensure international distribution with a focus on Africa. This international aspect is crucial for the designers, authors and photographers. The Fund and the Africa World Press would like to thank all these contributors for their enthusiasm and commitment.

Els van der Plas
Director of the Prince Claus Fund

PHOTOGRAPHERS
Karin Duthie, Gaborone, Botswana
Mamadou Touré Béhan, Dakar, Senegal
Bruno de Medeiros, Abidjan, Ivory Coast
Alain Herman, Paris, France
Eric Don-Arthur, Accra, Ghana

EDITORS
Els van der Plas
Marlous Willemsen

The Prince Claus Fund decided to pay tribute to African fashion and textiles. This fine initiative is gratifying for Africa as well as Europe, for it turns the spotlight on African talent, knowledge and know-how, both traditional and modern, which interweave to give shape, colour and life to our hope.

Long unfamiliar to the Western public except as occasional museum exhibits, African textiles began to penetrate the European fashion world in the 1980s. At the same time, Africa's capital cities were discovering a new type of entertainment: the fashion show, with its array of stars, clothes and models. It all began with the unforgettable, incomparable Chris Seydou (1949-1994, Mali). His fashion shows in Abidjan, Dakar, Bamako and elsewhere were simply breathtaking. More than anyone, he helped to give African men and women a new way of thinking, of looking at things, and inspired numerous designers and models to aim even higher.

In introducing the publication on African textiles and fashion, I believe consideration should be given to the deeper meaning, the development and the potential of this new dynamism.

Clothing is the message, and the clothed body is brimming with meaning, in Africa as elsewhere. Affluent, technological, standardised societies tend to forget the meaning of this twofold relationship between ourselves and our clothing and between the clothed body and other people (in the immediate vicinity or further away). Whether conventional, collusive or rebellious, clothing ultimately enables us to be ourselves with and among other people – sometimes the same as them, sometimes not. Clothing is the bearer of our, and society's, images of ourselves, of our desires and impulses.

Fashion comes into being as soon as a member of the community – a designer – creates something unusual which is taken up by the group and worn for some length of time. In Africa's present day context, in which its designers are drawing considerably on their cultural and historical heritage, fashion provides a link between past, present and future. It is a search for identity, an assertion and a projection into the future. It involves both being and appearing. In the past, appearing was subordinate to being, which continued to be of primary importance because it was imbued with the breath of life and communicated it to clothing as though it were a second skin. In many African societies, magicians and marabouts were, and still are, able to reach someone by handling a piece of clothing which the person has worn.

In addition to this profound, intimate, intimistic bond, clothing conveyed information about the wearer's age, sex, ethnic background and socio-economic status. The clothing, hairstyles and ornaments which Peul girls once wore, and in some circles still wear, distinguish them from Bozo or Bamana girls. Within each ethnic group, the bride's trousseau consists of clothing, which marks the passage to adulthood. In most cases the colours and patterns also convey messages and social values. Weddings, as well as births and funerals, are occasions for forming and consolidating social bonds by making gifts and counter-gifts of fabrics, as well as kitchen utensils for the bride.

The changes wrought by fashion in recent years have blurred national boundaries. The clothing traditions of the various ethnic groups and cultures are now shifting and interacting to create a new African aesthetic which includes an universal element. The people of coastal and central Africa now wear boubous and bogolan, while kente and raffia are now found in the countries of the Sahel. In industrialised Northern countries many consumers are now tempted by the colours and patterns of African textiles. At the same time, a new generation of designers – from tailors to renowned stylists – has emerged. Not content merely to reproduce models from imported fashion magazines, they now appropriate, reinterpret and transcend them with the help of local know-how and materials such as cotton, wool and fibre. In the course of this collective search for identity, African designers are also desperately seeking to be different, to find that special touch which will distinguish them from the rest. Alphadi (1957, Mali), Pathé O (1954, Ivory Coast), Claire Kane (1954, France), Lamine Kouyaté (1962d, Mali, label Xuly Bët) and Oumou Sy (1952, Senegal) are helping to write contemporary African and world history.

Such dynamism could, and should, have served to boost Africa's textile industries. While they did attempt to take advantage of it by printing traditional patterns, in most countries they then fell into a slump from which they are having great difficulty in recovering. If African fashion has survived this slump in the African textile industry relatively unscathed, it is because local craftspeople have vigorously withstood the cultural onslaught.

It is a good thing for Africa in general, and more particularly for its thousands of craftspeople (weavers, dyers, tailors, embroiderers), its stylists and its models, that the Prince Claus Fund is helping to broaden the horizons of African textiles and fashion. For this the Fund deserves our thanks.

Aminata Dramane Traoré
Minister of Culture and Tourism, Mali

Dress, design by Alphadi,
Niamey, Niger
© of the photographer,
Alain Herman, Paris, France

2

Visitor dressed for the occasion of a concert
of Baaba Maal, Cascas, Senegal
Courtesy of PAOPIM/KIT, Dakar,
Senegal/Amsterdam, the Netherlands

Sartorial ecumenes: African styles in a social and economic context

HUDITA NURA MUSTAFA

When you're well-dressed,
full of perfume, à la mode,
you feel good in your skin,
you feel good about yourself,
you can go anywhere.

Deinaba Ba
Senior civil servant, Dakar, Senegal

Shop signs on tailoring ateliers around Dakar announce 'Modu Diop, Maitre Tailleur', 'Pap Casset, Créateur' or 'Khady Sy, Touba Couture'. The trader, the couturière, the dirriankhe (a slang term for elegant, corpulent women), these are the new stars of Dakar's vibrant popular culture. Since the 1980s they have been dressing, or impressing, their clients, relatives and friends with some of the most stylish garments in West Africa. But how could this explosion of fashion have taken place during this period of financial instability?[1]

With the collapse of the neo-colonial institutions that were intended to create an African middle class, African institutions and practices have been revived and new niches have been opened up. Fashion, which is defined here as tailoring, object and image circulation and display, in fact results from the crisis and works as both strategy and expression. This essay shows how the rise of fashion interrelates potently with wider socio-economic and cultural restructurings and contestations, including intensified globalisation and large-scale power struggles. It will be examining the globalisation and massification of fashion in Dakar, Senegal, during the 1990s and the emergence of a design culture in South Africa in the post-1994 period. Fashion, I would suggest, is a domain for the negotiation of changing social relations, local institutions and transnational connections.

THE GLOBALISATION AND MASSIFICATION OF FASHION IN DAKAR, SENEGAL

Fashion in Senegal is an ironic phenomenon of expansion and instability, the intensification and undermining of inequality, local cultural autonomy and global economic dependence. Dakar's couturiers, the most diverse and renowned on the continent, are fabricating an African modernity that addresses the hybridities, contradictions and aspirations of the post-colonial condition. Modernity, as promised by colonial projects, has not delivered progress, rationality and well-being. Collapsing states, environmental degradation and economic malaise all make African failure seem inevitable.

Yet despair, anger and resistance as well as utopias and reinventions thrive in popular culture all over Africa. In contrast to the perversions involved in the transplanted neo-colonial institutions of state and economy, popular culture seems rooted in the popular economy and society. Painting in Congo, fashion in Dakar and music in Nigeria cannot be contained within the analytic confines of colonial dialectics, cultural imperialism and tradition or authenticity.

In the domain of fashion, we see links with some of the fundamental transformations of the modern epoch such as commodification, urbanisation and globalisation. Old circuits, ideas and practices have been reinvigorated, not extinguished. The African love of pageantry, adornment and social events and newer forms of media, industrial products and public spaces allow fashion to shape new cosmopolitan societies and identities. In conjunction with local ideals, institutions and material constraints, global fashion forms what I would call a sartorial ecumene. This ecumene is pronounced in urban zones as it is here that global flows and media shape society most forcefully. Here also,

15

6

Dirriankhes at a Xew, Dakar, Senegal
Courtesy of Hudita Nura Mustafa

Diongoma contest, June 1993,
Dakar, Senegal, left Josephine,
right Fata Sow, hairdresser
Courtesy of Hudita Nura Mustafa

anonymity and heterogeneity enable a fluidity of the public self, which can be created in part through appearance. It is through the definition of sartorial ecumenes that we may examine and distinguish diverse cosmopolitanisms and identify modern, African fashion systems.

Dakar is a special case because it has been a trading, administrative and cultural centre of West Africa and Francophone Africa since the colonial period. Lagos, Ibadan and Abidjan also have thriving design cultures, all building on long histories of cloth-making and use. In East and Southern Africa, the fashion culture is much less developed, although consumption continues to be key to social status. In these regions, Christianity has worked to repress local dress practices. In Dakar, urban middle classes, and not elites, have been at the core of the explosion of fashion. Through them, fashion has been key to the response to economic crisis and to expressions of ambivalence about social change and moral decay. In Dakar in particular, in accordance with a long-standing tradition of representing beauty as honour, women play a crucial role in the exchange, display and discourses of the sartorial ecumene.

The spectacular garments and arresting individuals that populate Dakar's public spaces illustrate the vital importance of appearance, dress and beauty there. Not only are the people, and especially the women, strikingly beautiful, but they are fashionable, and pay all the attention to conduct, style and detail that this entails. A trip to the post office is a lesson in the contradictions of modernity.

Just imagine the following scene. At a busy corner on the edge of a posh district housing the university, embassies and the beginning of the middle class suburbs is the post-office. You cross a dry garden and enter the unremarkable concrete building from the noisy, dusty streets. Long lines of customers wait their turn to be served by a small number of clerks. The paint on the wall is flaking, counters are dusty from winter sands, and the post office clerk takes her time. Upon arrival at the head of the queue, you present your pile of letters to her. She barely looks at you. It's as if your requirements are too trifling and petty for her. She takes the pile with measure, carefully weighs each letter on a manual scale, and calculates the postage cost with a calculator, always careful not to damage her perfectly manicured nails.

Her face is a perfect mask of cosmetic colours: navy blue eyeliner, burgundy eye shadow highlighted with copper, and dark red lipstick that match her embroidered robe. The phone rings, she greets her friend with the combination of gusto and reserve required of women: 'Khadi, nga def, comment ça va, nga def....je donnerai quinze mille, en lieu de facture eau bi' (which is French and Wolof for 'Khady, how are you?... I am going to give 15,000 instead of paying the water bill'). Overhearing this conversation, you realise that she is preparing to go to a naming ceremony. As the conversation continues, you try to identify her perfume. Is it Chanel or Estée Lauder? After a few minutes, she hangs up and returns to your letters. She adjusts her robe so that it sits perfectly balanced on her shoulders. The whole chest area of her dress is embroidered with multi-coloured arabesques. The dark green, navy and gold colours complement the royal blue cloth, or are they too bright? Finally, nonchalantly, she tells you how much you need to pay: '750 cfa (1 USD = 555 CFA [1998]). You barely hear, as you are absorbed in the twirls of the embroidery, wondering if it was made in a market or a fancy shop. It certainly looks good, but the thread is already frayed. It can't be French silk. She repeats the words '750 CFA', this time with a tone that suggests a little annoyance. You awaken from your self-absorbed curiosity and pay her. You make your way back to the noisy streets and the next customer moves forward. You know that your letter will arrive on time, but you still wonder how such women can juggle their small salaries with their social and sartorial needs.

At a historical conjuncture marked by transformations in the institutions of popular culture and rapid changes in social relations of age, gender and class, a vivid play with cosmopolitan identity formation has crystallised in fashion. Fashion is a frontier of struggle among colonial civilising projects, African self-representation, local power contests and the collective shaping of specific modernities. Can such a phenomenon be reduced to an effect of the colonial encounter, tutelage by and competition with French masters or a rebellion against the legacies of apartheid? Can it be reduced to status rivalry? To sexualisation and commodification for the marriage market? How do the two quotes that accompany this essay, and the scene at the post office just described, illuminate a specifically African fashion practice? For the young South African designer, fashion hierarchicises on the basis of first use of new styles. The Senegalese woman speaks of the creation of a powerful, public self through dress. These comments indicate the coexistence of long-standing African self-making practices based on bodily adornment, and modern fashion, which is a system of social differentiation based on the rapid circulation and imitation of objects and images. The vignette illustrates the way that these practices merge in women's interpenetrating ceremonial, work and social lives. For our clerk, fashion means participating in commercialised, rivalrous displays that have always been at the core of the African social fabric. The desires for the new, the expensive, the exotic, and the eyes of all are fuelled by intensifying transnational flows.

OLD AND NEW COSMOPOLITANISMS

There is nothing new about cosmopolitanism in Africa. Venetian glass bead necklaces, the use of tomato paste in cooking and the custom of speaking Arabic are all evidence of long histories of conquest, conversion, trade and appropriation. Layers of influence from Wolof status systems to Islam, French colonialism and US mass culture permeate material culture, especially dress. Billowing boubous, embroidered robes that are recognised all over the world as being traditionally West African, are far from authentic, if authentic is defined in terms of location and origin. This Arab style spread with Islamic conversion from the eighteenth century and is now at the pinnacle of dress in Islamic societies. The cloth is imported from Europe and Asia. Such objects and images of the Dakar fashion system provide a rich repertoire for material expressions of cultural ideals, individual excellence and collective tradition. The signature of Dakar fashion, more than in many

Well dressed woman, Dakar, Senegal
Courtesy of Hudita Nura Mustafa

other places, is diversity of style, hybridity and an unrelenting capacity to appropriate. In addition, many Senegalese women of all strata simply have an awe-inspiring natural elegance of physical appearance and carriage. 'We learned it from our grandmothers', they say, and they know that their beauty is read as a sign of familial dignity.

The modern fashion system in the Senegalese context is a merging of global fashion circulations and local institutions and meanings to form what I have termed a sartorial ecumene. An ecumene brings together images and goods from differing cultural and geographical origins in new combinations. By a sartorial ecumene I mean the incorporation of objects and images of global origins into practices and circulations involving dress and bodily adornment. In Africa, the exchange of cloth through gifts, loans, savings groups and other financial practices enables dress and fashion to flourish. Popular cultural institutions such as dance events organised for women, weekend balls and concerts are all occasions for dressing up. New media such as television and photography intensify the circulation of fashion. In Dakar in particular, the inflation and frequency of ritual gift exchange and self-display, crisis strategies and the rise of fashion and the cloth trade have reinforced each other since the 1980s. The analytical lens of the sartorial ecumene enables the observer to see multiple restructurings that not only create new dependencies, but also destabilise current neo-colonial and local class domination. The sartorial ecumene reinforces old and new dependencies within the global economy.

In this context, two powerful trends have been in evidence in Senegal. First of all, there has been a reorientation away from the colonial dimension towards a global ecumene. Secondly, this shift coincides with the emergence of a Mouride mercantile, urban class. The neo-colonial elites of the four communes were shaped through education as civilised black Frenchmen. Elegance was part of this and the members of the elites had to have a new dress at start of the new season or risk being branded as ignoramuses. Urban supremacy is deeply rooted. However, as the foundations of this urban elite and middle class are eroded in the wake of the decline in education and employment, Islamic and North American connections emerge as the Mourides seek viable commercial and cultural links to shore up their national prominence. It is thanks to the cheap East Asian imitations of damask, prints and the sheer cotton, khartoum, that fashion has become democratised. While Europe remains a source of luxury cloth, Nigeria and East Asia are now key sources of cheaper cloth, accessories and primary materials such as threads, reinforcements and linings. Such a range of qualities and prices has opened up fashion as a terrain not just for the urban elite, but anyone with some cash, or a gift of cloth and a good tailor.

HISTORICAL CROSS-CULTURAL EXCHANGE

The location of Senegambia on the edge of desert, savannah and ocean make it a prime spot for cross-cultural exchange. The combination of competition for control over politics, religion and trade has led to a very turbulent history involving European, Islamic and African societies. Since the fourth century it has been connected to other regions of Africa such as the Sahel and the forest zones. Food, salt, cloth and gold were traded among Africans. Europeans began trading in the region in the tenth century. Portuguese and, later, British and French vessels plied the coast and competed for access to trade markets there. The seventeenth and eighteenth centuries were periods of heightened trade, the collapse of the Wolof state systems and the spread of Islam. By 1890, the French were in political control on the coast and consolidated their rule over West Africa by means of military conquests.

A number of examples can be cited to illustrate the prominent uses of cloth in this history. Until the French conquest, white strip cloth woven by casted weavers was a medium of exchange in parts of Senegambia, especially along the Senegal river. Made in heavy threads and colours, it was, and still is, a luxury item. In fact, cloth was among the items used to buy the slaves and gum, which were so crucial to Europe's economic development. At the end of the eighteenth century, the instability in the region was such that a slave could be bought for a length of strip cloth on the streets of the major port, St. Louis. Another form of cloth currency, the guinée, an indigo length produced in the French Indian colony of Pondicherry, was introduced by the French during the 1800s. It soon became a preferred cloth because of its quality and was used by the French to buy food during their military conquest of the interior of Sahelian Africa. Even today, guinée is used as a name for indigo dyed cloth. In the 1800s, British and Dutch industries designed printed, cheaper cloth specifically to capture the African market. The proliferation of types of cloth actually helped to undermine local hand-woven production. In more recent times, the control over the cloth trade was a key part of colonial policy. This was done through the 'économie de traîte', in which trading firms monopolised the marketing of peasants' peanut production and paid them with store credit for French goods. Cloth accounted for some of the biggest expenditure. The post-war 'pacte coloniale' integrated colony and metropole economically, educationally and militarily. It provided a monopolised market for French interests, including the textile industry, in the wake of the wartime slump. In short, the production of hand-crafted cloth was undermined throughout the colonial period in favour of European industry.

THE UPS AND DOWNS OF THE DOMESTIC TEXTILE INDUSTRY

While the domestic textile industry has floundered, the textile trade has flourished. The Société de Textile in Senegal, Sotiba, has been confronted with problems such as changing ownership, mismanagement and use again as a market for expensive French inputs. It was only saved by state subsidies. One of its main challenges has been that it can match neither the exoticism and high quality of European cloth nor the low cost of Asian cloth. In 1998, the per metre cost of cotton prints was CFA 600 for Asian prints, CFA 3,000 for European prints and CFA 1,000 for domestic prints. Damask was CFA 6,000 for the Austrian 'basin riche' or CFA 2,000 for East Asian 'false' damask. A six-metre length of Swiss voile cost CFA 15,000 in 1993, a jacarde boubou cost CFA 25,000

Men in the street, Benin
Courtesy of Vlisco BV, Helmond
the Netherlands

and a really luxurious boubou cost between CFA 40,000 and CFA 60,000. Imitations of these cost about half the price.

At a time when the industry was facing closure in the late 1980s, the newly established Sotiba marketing team set about conquering the urban market, which had hitherto regarded its cloth as rural and for old people. It sponsored cloth inputs and televised fashion contests for local producers. The result was a plethora of highly innovative, splendid women's garments and invaluable publicity for local designers. The aim was to promote Sotiba products as modern, affordable, fashionable and cosmopolitan. The campaign worked, and Sotiba cloth and Euro-African fashion was popularised among young, urban middle-class women.

Imports are still important at the highest (i.e. most profitable) and lowest (i.e. most numerous) levels of consumption. Since the 1980s, the contemporary trade regime has been characterised by an extension of trading networks and a diversification and Africanisation of the field. French trading firms and Lebanese middlemen monopolised commerce up to and beyond 1960, when Senegal was granted its full independence. Since the 1980s, women, mostly Wolofs, have dominated the wholesale cloth trade. They travel to manufacturers in Austria, Switzerland and the Netherlands, and to whole-salers in Saudi Arabia for luxury damasks, voiles, jacardes and brocades. Major Senegalese wholesalers engage Hong Kong manufacturers to produce imitations of luxury cloth for the low-income market.

Retailers and suitcase traders travel to other locations. The United States is a source of blue jeans and T-shirts, cosmetics, wigs and baseball caps. Las Palmas and Italy are sources of garments and accessories such as leather goods, flashy gold-finished slippers and purses. Gambia, whose border is closed by law but is open in practice, is a source of cheap Asian cloth. Many of all these kinds of goods are actually produced in East Asia, although Nigeria is gaining in importance as a source of cloth, cosmetics and sewing accessories. Although the markets in Sandaga are important centres of the cloth trade, suitcase traders disseminate goods within social networks and sell on credit with monthly payments ranging from CFA 1 to CFA 10,000. Women traders have pioneered the selling of Senegalese garments overseas to fellow traders, pilgrims in Jeddah and to the Senegalese diaspora in Europe and the USA. Such trade is organised through religious, especially Mouride, networks and corruption at borders, where, thanks to marabouts' connections, customs officials are bribed to reduce taxes.

Compared to cloth consumption, the domain of tailoring, on the other hand is one in which local talent and production are highly valorised. Unlike other African contexts, such as Abidjan or Johannesburg, the designer label is not crucial to the desirability of a garment. Since the 1970s, the low capital and high demand involved in tailoring have made it a niche for steady expansion, diversification and conflict. According to official estimates, there are about 3,300 ateliers located along Dakar's main commercial roads. By my estimate there are at least 7,000 tailors. While the stitching of cloth lengths into robes and wraps has a long history, sewing machines have only been

Women selling fabrics, Benin
Courtesy of Vlisco BV, Helmond
the Netherlands

used for the past century or so. The first trained African tailors learned to sew in French colonial military and medical institutions. They then trained their relatives through an apprenticeship system. Tailoring expanded dramatically in the 1970s with the influx of young rural men into urban zones following droughts and agricultural decline.

In the 1980s, unemployment hit middle-class men as the state and companies downsized. Urban middle-class women entered tailoring as entrepreneurs, hired male tailors and relied on their social networks for financial support and clientele. Thanks to the lively trade in used sewing machines from Europe, the price of such machines fell to as low as CFA 30,000. In the 1990s, women began to lead the field and faced increasing hostility from male artisans, who claimed that untrained women are not legitimate craftspersons. As competition has increased, so has creativity in style. All producers claim to be designers and innovate in order to attract clients. Women in particular use their designer status to reinvent their work identities as they enter a low status, manual occupation. Design has also become a highly collaborative process in which the tailor and the client work closely together, consulting both media sources and friends. Prices have fallen such that, in 1993, a medium-range large embroidery could be bought for CFA 7,000, a taille-basse for CFA 5,000 and a skirt suit for as little as CFA 3,000. An average small businessperson's monthly salary was CFA 35,000 whilst a top-level bureaucrat living in a city with a high cost of living and under tremendous pressure to help others financially would be earning around CFA 100,000.

THE EMERGENCE OF THE 'ORDINARY' COSMOPOLITANS

The terrains of trade, tailoring and fashion consumption flourished on account of the urgency of middle-class needs for income generation. New cultural producers and brokers whom I have designated as 'ordinary cosmopolitans' have emerged from such phenomena. Shaped through institutions of popular culture and economy, not schools, they are active consumers who reconstitute objects and images according to local lexicons. They may wear African dress on Fridays, slinky attire for a Saturday evening ball, and jogging suits when they sell goods in the market place. They fund their consumption and familial duties through savings groups or ceremonial circulations and loans. The naming of styles after popular music, celebrities, places or television characters or even friends is an example of such cultural activity. For instance, Alexis, the infamous character from Dynasty, the American television series, is used as a name for the long, slit skirt which has also been popular in European fashion for several years. In 1993, Yow Lele was the title of a Youssou Ndour song which was a modern version of an old Pulaar ballad. It was also the name of a taille basse style and a revival of a Peul hairstyle. During the same years, Naomi Campbell, light years away from Pulaar song, lent her name to a long wig. This was called 'cheveux indiens' and was worn, appropriately, with an Indian saree borrowed from a Hindi film.

This kind of circulation indicates a new density of public culture in which the media, social life and the ease of artisanal production promote styles. They are reinforced by this circulation, which also allows for popular intervention as when, for instance, tailors take their inspiration from songs. In this culture of celebrity, social events and street life also circulates style. At weddings and naming days, everyone watches the neighbourhood fashion queens for signs of the latest cloth from Jeddah or the newest embroidery thread. As I became used to street life, I also learned to read the street for waves of fashion in colour, cut and cloth. During the Id-ul-Hajj of 1993, Swiss voile was very in, especially among young women. By 1998, it was considered outmoded and its delicate beauty was of little interest.

MAPPING THE WORLD WITH STYLE

Style is a veritable mapping of the world onto Dakar popular culture. Yet the lexicon of dress revolves around a dichotomy of traditional/African and European/tubaab (the Wolof word for foreigner) which misrepresents the hybridity of Dakar style. African dress comprises the embroidered boubou, an Islamic dress adopted in the last two centuries, and the taille basse and ndockette, both European styles from the coastal trading zones. European dress includes trousers, shirts, dresses, skirts and jackets. Cloth also extends hybridity as African prints are used to make European or hybrid styles. Unquestionably, though, the boubou, as an African dress, is the pinnacle of prestige and beauty. It is a requisite for religious holidays and familial ceremonies which are the centre of community attention. As an additional point, women's fashion has emerged as the mainstream of production and hybrid design. Men's fashion is largely limited to Western suits, hip-hop style and boubous, with little change except in embroidery. Dakar fashion represents a modernity of reinvention, hybridity and ambivalence towards both European and elitist models of modernity. In this model of modernity, 'ordinary cosmopolitans' emerge as the arbiters of transnational connections shaped through the contestation of European hegemony, and local gender, class and age hierarchies.

This cosmopolitanism creatively localises global goods and images. Used curtains are turned into ball gowns. Exaggeratedly applied face powder is used as a mask. Blue jeans culture thrives as part of the imported US rap culture, but is also connected to local music and anti-state youth culture. The work of fuug jaay tailors (tailors working with disdained second-hand clothing that is commercialised in Africa) irreverently bastardises the esteemed 'costume', a symbol of the civilised African man, the 'fonctionnaire' with his overstarched collar. Imported, used suits are cut up, decorated with badges or trims to make up-to-the-minute jackets for young people. Worn with baggy Sotiba print trousers by a 20-year-old minibus conductor, its transformation is in defiance of the suit's official pretensions. Indeed, the sartorial ecumene of recycling, gift-giving and display institutionalises a cosmopolitanism that advocates African autonomy yet avidly incorporates foreign elements.

The contrast between traditional and European styles forms a good starting point for describing the relationship between context, style, age and propriety, the major principles of dress convention. Briefly, European dress is acceptable for European-type contexts such as offices and downtown shopping. In practice, married women stop wearing Western dress after they have their first child unless they frequent offices. Men stop wearing European dress in their fifties. In addition, Western dress is associated with youth, a low-status social position, limited Western contexts and fuug jaay. Traditional dress is an absolute necessity for familial ceremonies and religious holidays The exception is weddings, which comprise both religious events for men in the morning and evening receptions for the bride and her friends. For the reception, brides don white dresses or taille basses in expensive satins and taffetas and elaborate coiffures. Guests present wrapped gifts, and cakes and soft drinks are served.

Modesty, based on Islamic ideals, is a major principle in dress and the related issue of conduct. At the same time, the boubou and ndockette are worn to conceal by means of volume, while also suggesting underlying physical form through movement. To give an example, I was actually exhorted to walk slowly and with the hips when I adopted Senegalese clothes. A very low boubou neckline, hanging off the shoulders, was in vogue during the eighties, but would today be regarded as indecent and a sign of a low social status and/or a lack of moral standards. Once a woman reaches a certain state of portliness after childbearing, it is seen as neither proper nor attractive for her to wear fitted exposing garments. I myself have heard people criticise married women in their late thirties for wanting to wear skirts all the time and so 'play at being young'. Children, as is so often the case, manoeuvre to circumvent the rules. One friend explained to me matter of factly that whenever her grandmother, who wears multiple layers of hand-woven wrap, berates her for wearing miniskirts, she simply wears a wrap to go out. Upon arrival at a friend's house, she discards it before proceeding to her Saturday evening ball.

The concern with modesty does not translate into Islam-inspired veiling. In fact, most Senegalese consider both form-fitted clothing and veiling to be un-African. During a vociferous argument between a mother and her veiled daughter, the daughter, a member of one of the Islamic movements that have grown since the 1980s, claimed that the Koran requires the entire body to be covered. Although the mother insisted that this was not part of their tradition, she admitted that she could do nothing to stop her child, and relented. Veiled women do, however, keep abreast of certain trends in fashion by buying the colours of the season, seeking tailors who can compose original designs and wearing matching accessories. If married, they like alluring underwear as much as other women.

Hybridity does not mean simply exchanging fashions with the West and the Islamic world, however. There is a great deal of regional borrowing in Senegal. The Mauritanian mulf and the Beninois two-wraps were introduced by trading communities in Mauritania and Benin. The former is sheer cotton, six metres in length, wrapped around the body and head. The latter is in African print, one a long skirt, the other hip-hugging with a top. Among traditional cloth, hand-dyed damask, the best quality of which is from Mali, is highly esteemed. In fact, it is regarded as being so

Woman in a ndockette, Dakar, Senegal
Courtesy of Hudita Nura Mustafa

Alexis, design by Vlisco BV,
Helmond, the Netherlands

beautiful, with or without patterns, that it is usually worn without embroidery. It is the ultimate in tradition. And yet a young, educated Toucouleur woman commented in my presence that, although she preferred imported voile, 'our relatives, they're not intellectuals; they only wear tuub.'

The political elite has also played a role in recent challenges to the hegemony of European dress in urban public life. During Senghor's rule (1956-1981), suits were de rigueur for male members of the elite. Since the early 1980s, President Abdou Diouf and his entourage have vied with leading marabouts as if enacting political struggles symbolically. Everyone watches televised events or mosque visits on religious holidays and talks about the ten-metre boubous complete with trousers, tunic and covering robes that are canvasses for the richest embroidery on the continent. These are the products of Douma Diakhate, Ba Sene and Dan Fall; just a few of Dakar's couturiers who cater for African heads of state. A limited Islamic revival in the observance of Friday dress and prayers has also popularised African dress. Even as trade networks diversify, styles such as the boubou or ndockette have thrived since the 1980s and are valorised as authentically African.

THE FEMININE INFLUENCE

While women are culturally responsible for the preservation of family, tradition and honour, they have emerged as the most active negotiators of crisis and of transnationalism. For example, my friend Muesly, 27, is from a devout Mouride trading family from the interior with little French education. She assists her sister in a Dakar market cloth shop. This divorced sister supports a household of fifteen in addition to helping others. On Sunday afternoons, even if she is just intending to visit neighbours, she coifs her hair, dons the latest skirt suit or an old boubou and as usual treats herself with body lotion. She admires Alexis' toughness as a businesswoman, and, although she disapproves of her sexual promiscuity, her bulging wardrobe also contains Alexis skirts with slits in the front, side and back. At the same time, her passion is African dress and she has three albums with portraits of herself in ceremonial dress. This household provides garment loans, hand-me-downs and gifts from their tailors to the extended family. If she marries an immigrant trader, she will become one of the wealthiest and most elegant women in her neighbourhood, outshining the daughters of professors, but still incurring their disdain for her flashy style.

Young women like Muesly are at the core of high-pace Euro-African fashion and European styles of skirt outfits. They rely on gifts of cloth and money from parents or suitors. During holidays, they expect to buy CFA 5,000 worth of hair extensions or a wig, as well as cloth for sewing into clothes. They may make a last-minute attempt to gather CFA 3,000 more for shoes and CFA 2,000 for a purse. They lend each other garments either for their own use or for copying by tailors. Their taille basse style displays their concern with feminine form, and perhaps fertility. The tight skirt and the fanciful torso highlight an African preference for the hips and the neck/shoulder area. In the late 1980s, several elaborate sleeve styles had re-emerged in Paris, such as the ballooning Marie Antoinette and multi-petaled flowers. Tailors and clients alike peruse journals and modify Parisian models to make what they call 'creations' of sleeves, asymmetrical necklines and other surprises. This sector of fashion has plenty of examples not only of the commodi-fication of women for the marriage market, but also of the very real self-making, according to long-standing African ideals, of tailors, women and families in the face of uncertainty.

Finally, hair presents one of the most dynamic fashion hybrids involving the long-standing aesthetic ideals and newer global, industrial products. All over Africa, the head is a repository of the power of body, mind and spirit. Braiding has been a hair care and beautification practice for as long as one can recall, and is especially intricate in West Africa. Since the 1970s, synthetic hair has replaced wool as a means of extending length and thickness for designs and wig-making. This hair is of Korean origin, and is made in Dakar or imported from New York. Alongside tailoring, hair salons have been a major arena for middle-class investment. While older women wear simple braids and scarves, younger women can use the whole range and often prefer fancy braids or wigs.

PAGEANTRY, POWER AND IMITATION

Pageantry has always been crucial to the definition, exertion and contestation of power in Africa. In ritual contexts, key players in the spirit world or state power perform and publicly reaffirm their power through dress display. Prestigious dress, as with the exercise of power more broadly, represents the capacity to mobilise material resources, productive labour and a community of recognition. The regalia of Ashanti kings with their tremendous gold bangles and the multiple swathes of woven cloth worn by pre-colonial Wolof aristocracy are vivid reminders of their wealth and power. Throughout Africa, artisans are linked hierarchically to courts or important families. Thus, the moment of pageantry crystallises a society's aesthetic and social values and hierarchies.

In today's Senegal, the beauty of objects and people incites powerful emotions of admiration and desire, rivalry and ambivalence. Gold jewellery, luxury cloth and regal conduct are still the ideals of beauty. Old proverbs warn against admiring beauty at the expense of goodness, yet, in practice, beauty is seen as a kind of goodness. The topical issue at the moment is the source of wealth and beauty. Is the most expensive cloth the most beautiful? What sacrifices were made to finance that dress? Who dresses for whom? And should it really be so very important? The minutiae of style make it forceful for both inculcation into and contestation of domination. Contemporary African fashion relies on local proclivities towards bodily adornment, current economies of circulation and key social restructurings. In South Africa, both the white media and black politicians proclaim that the new South African black elite is squandering money on Escada at a time when the children in Soweto have no schoolbooks. In Senegal, dirriankhes are denounced in music as well as in everyday discourse for dressing themselves in the latest boubou while their children eat porridge. Yet, everyone is keen to find out whose boubou was the most spectacular at a particular event and whether it was a good copy of the President's wife's. Such are the contradictions of modern pageantry. The ruses of ordinary people's pageantry, 'sanse' (the Wolof

word for fancy dress), are imitation and valorisation. Ordinary tailors and their clients take their stylistic leads from ceremonies and television celebrities. For them, East Asian cloth doubles as Austrian damask, and Nigerian polyester thread as French silk embroidery threads. Trims of eyelet lace, embroidery, appliqués, or painting augment the beauty and value of cheap cloth. Simple embroidery is now in vogue in deliberate opposition to the former fashion of ostentation, but the aim remains to make cheap cloth look expensive. As one friend explained to me about a necklace made of gold polyester beads, 'it looks like gold from a distance'. For instance, gold-spun embroidery thread for boubous was introduced by a well-off woman who brought Pakistani tailors to Dakar and charged CFA 20,000 in 1993. Within six months, this had been copied by elite Dakar designers and then by neighbourhood tailors who, as cheaper thread was found and imported, were willing to sell it for CFA 7,000. Tailors are inspired by cloth motifs to produce embroidery patterns and so create original garments.

The boubou, once the dress of powerful men, marabouts and princes, today indicates the redistribution of symbolic power through gender as well as income groups. Display is seen as a practice of disguise and even false pretensions and fallen morals. This is often a gendered critique which poses dress as narcissism and disregard of familial duty, often linked with prostitution or sexual promiscuity. It reflects an ambivalence towards the new mobility of small businesswomen and their role as the sole breadwinner in a household. Similar ambivalences exist around the familial ceremonies (xew in Wolof) that form a major site of pageantry. Since the 1980s, both old and new elites have used ostentatious weddings and naming ceremonies as a means of displaying their wealth and competing with each other. Ordinary people follow suit in the name of tradition or honour, relying on savings, community aid, loans and enormous sacrifice. These events are organised by and for female in-laws. In earlier times these were generally feasts to which kin and neighbours contributed and modest amounts of cloth were given to key relatives. Cloth, as a gift embodying the giver's spirit, was meant to bind social ties. Individual happiness went hand-in-hand with the celebration of community, it is now claimed. Today, the success of a day of feasting, dress, dancing and ritual gift exchange is measured by the quantity of gift exchange and by the number of guests and the dress which they choose to wear. Even middle-class women feel that they cannot wear a robe more than four times and must then relegate it to casual wear or to a relative. The risk is that their peers would consider them to be in financial trouble or disregarded by their husbands. Xew are, in effect, as much fashion contests and wealth circulation as community consolidation.

In 1994, after the CFA had been devalued by fifty percent, one of the wealthiest female traders 'baptised' her daughter after the first child's birth. Brocades from Switzerland, hand-dyed damasks from Mali, Pakistani gold and floral embroidery formed a dazzling ocean of colour. Gold necklaces hung heavily around necks and shoulders, both luxury and chains. The universal wearing of elaborate headscarves declared that this was an important event. To arrive in such a sea of

'Uniqueness, new things that come up on a regular basis, moving from one place to the next; when people come up to you, you have to be above, be ahead. That's what I regard as fashion.'

Helen Taylor, young black designer,
Johannesburg, South Africa

elegance required aplomb. The wealthiest arrived in a chauffeur-driven Mercedes flanked by an entourage of outriders. The first few younger women cleared a path through the guests as the dirriankhes followed, grasping the trains of their robes. Walking at a cultivated stride, they slowly crossed the central area on their high-heeled slippers with lengths of luxury cloth tracing the movements of their portly bodies. Whilst remaining keenly aware of other people's gazes, they deliberately acted as nonchalantly as possible, desperate as they were to create an impression that they were not actually looking at anyone at all. Even as, literally overnight, most families changed their diets to cheaper foods, rumours began to arise that forty million CFA had been circulated and that the sanse was among the finest in recent times. Today's pageantry, of rich or poor, is embedded in tensions surrounding the relationship between the individual and his or her community, the commercialisation of social life and the meaning of pageantry.

FASHION AND POST-APARTHEID SOUTH AFRICAN CULTURAL POLITICS

The democratic transition in post-1994 South Africa has fostered a lively debate on culture and identity. President-elect Mbeki has declared this to be the era of African Renaissance. Following the honeymoon after the first elections, the interpretation of the national identity as a rainbow is now up for debate, as assertions of ethnic identity and impatience with race and class privilege begin to emerge. As they move away from a legacy of protest art, cultural producers are now grappling with the problem of how to build new identities and a national culture. Fashion illuminates these struggles for a place for individual expression, for race and class equity, for the revival of African sources for South African identity and for an engagement with global economic and cultural arenas. Since the first democratic elections in 1994, fashion has rapidly emerged on many fronts. The current design scene comprises established and young designers and is segregated by race, clientele and style of production. White designers follow European form and innovate with fabric combinations and style. A handful of black designers produce 'ethnic' clothing for the growing black elite. Fashion weeks (as held in 1997) and the SAFDA (South African Fashion Designers Association) Vukani awards (which have been in operation since 1994) suggest an emergent culture of design. In addition, major fashion magazines such as Elle and Ebony have established themselves in the past few years. Finally, courses in design at technical colleges are growing in popularity.

One of the greatest challenges facing South Africans is cultural recovery from the fascism and racism of the apartheid state and society. In fashion, the struggle to affirm individuality and African-ness is a guiding principle, in addition of course to the struggle for business survival. As Dion Chang, the fashion editor of Elle magazine, hopes, 'the spirit of individuality helps people cope with different race and culture groups... If there are thousands of piercings, they're not thugs, they're just expressing themselves'. Christian missionisation was a thoroughgoing civilising project that initiated Western religion and education as well as manners, dress and hygiene.

For Africans, any individual revival has to be coupled with a reconstruction of the African identity as well as a transformation from a culture of protest to a culture of national reconstruction. The search for an affirmation of Africanness has long been mediated by the appropriation of other African cultures. The US media enjoyed a monopoly during the period in which sanctions were in force, and black township society, long inspired by African American culture and politics, especially jazz, turned to rap and hip-hop culture. Long, blonde braids, baggy jeans, baseball caps and sports' gear define the youth scene. The Mandelas, First Lady Graca Machel and other leaders have promoted African fashion by wearing it as their official dress. Many black designers, including the Nigerian Fred Eboya, produce West African fashion which is adopted in South Africa as 'ethnic' or 'traditional' dress. Other designers reject West African dress as inappropriate for South Africans, who should instead seek internal inspiration.

Since 1988, the SAFDA has attempted to support young black designers with training and business advice. With the aid of government support, it has been able to begin an exploration of international markets. According to President Ndamasa, most people left school through politics and now find themselves in leadership. 'To someone who hasn't been to school, a suit is just a heavy garment. With the diversification of politics – thank God Mandela took over – you can now dress according to who you are.' SAFDA's Vukani awards for a national costume address this identity issue. Themes so far have included ethnic traditions, the new flag and national languages. Ndamasa's aim is to 'stop using Gucci and Yves St. Laurent, and instead to use the indigenous look to meet the international world. The world is looking for new ideas and is no longer interested in duplicates... Fabric must come from who you are.' As in Senegal, efforts to forge a cultural autonomy must face up to the reality of a dependence on imported goods. Lycras, stretch gauze and chiffons that fill Parisian and local fashion are imported.

Zulu and Ndebele beadwork is to Southern Africa what cloth is to West-African aesthetics and society. As the core of experiments in creating a distinctive South African fashion, it is used on headdresses, bodices and aprons. For Marian Fassler, the grande dame of South African design, it is not just a question of designing a token headdress or print, but shaping a silhouette that must be African. Working for twenty years and now with an international clientele, Fassler's trademark is leopard-print fabric, an echo of the leopard skin in pre-colonial Zulu regalia. She also uses beadwork and flowing silhouettes. In another irony of what stands for African in South Africa, 'traditional' dresses may well be the results of colonial encounters. Herero dress in Namibia is nineteenth century German dress and Xhosa dress is remarkably similar. Zulu dress is still grounded in pre-colonial styles of leather skirts and headdresses.

Conspicuous consumption is common across racial and income groups in South Africa. As in Senegal, debt and savings associations finance consumption outside monthly budgets.

Collection Hein Reiders, winner of the 1996 sales house annual Vukani Fashion Award, SAFDA, South African Fashion Designers Association, Johannesburg, South Africa
Courtesy of SAFDA, 1996

The prevalence of Mercedes and other luxury cars on South African roads is immediately evident. Whilst sanctions isolated South Africa from many global trends for years, this isolation did not result in the creation of a local fashion industry as the economic crisis has done in Senegal. The enormously wealthy white elite, and a small black elite, was able to travel and favoured European designer labels. Elite South African designers such as Marian Fassler, Errol Arendz and Norman Callan produce elaborate evening gowns and occasion wear that are European in form and fabric. Even for these elite designers, though, Europe no longer remains an unchallenged source of inspiration. No longer can elite South Africans pretend to be living in a mini-London. The black middle classes also promise to be a new market in the making, whose financial and aesthetic agendas are linked to larger national projects of transformation and a rejection of white supremacy.

THE EMERGENCE OF AFRICAN HAUTE COUTURE

A distinctly African haute couture has been emerging since the 1970s. This trend builds upon centuries-old traditions of cloth use and bodily adornment. Hence the prominence of West Africans in the field. They engage history to create a hybrid, urban modernity. They use woven, dyed, and embroidered cloth, even combined in a single garment. Forms vary from drapes and volume to the classic focus on head and shoulders. The late Chris Seydou (1949-1994, Mali) pioneered the use of the bogolan, Malian 'mud cloth', for Western styles. In Dakar, Kolle Ardo Sow, Claire Kane and Aïssa Dione all use woven cloth for garments, Western or African-inspired styles. The work of Oumou Sy directly recreates the dress of kings and queens. Alphadi's gowns and suits are spectacles of multiple textures – heavy woven cloth with voile – with suits, or form-fitting bustiers with flowing skirts. In cities like Abidjan and Dakar, throughout the ranks of designers and artisans, there is an excellence in using 'African fabrics' (i.e. imported prints and damasks, woven and dyed cloth) for all kinds of styles. In this regard, Joël Andrianomearisoa (Madagascar) is a rebel in his use of very 'modern' plastic-looking fabrics and body-baring styles in simple cuts. The challenge of creating new forms that transcend combinations remains here as in Europe. However, fashion's newness is often a revival of the old and perhaps we need to remember the past in order to move forward into the future.

The economic crisis which has engulfed the continent since the 1980s has had various effects. In many cases, used Western clothing has become ever more popular. In Nigeria, local tailors thrived when imported ready-to-wear clothing became costly. In Senegal, tailoring became income generation for the middle classes and the mask offered by clothing became crucial as financial instability intensified. The challenge now lies with creating an haute couture that caters for ruling elites as well as for the modest salaries of the professional classes.

The relationship between artisanal production, mass production and haute couture also needs to be investigated, without automatically assuming that industrial projects are bound to be the most attractive option. The issue of textile and sewing and fashion accessory importation is of urgent concern. There is also a pressing need to use the media to promote local producers and to forge a link between various forms of culture, as the music videos in Senegal do, for instance. Similarly, the fashion show as an art form has great promise, and could be integrated into multimedial, African forms of display. The excellent magazines coming out of Abidjan and South Africa could also be used to debate current political and cultural issues, as the South African magazines are attempting. Fashion is embedded in African community life and it should be exploited as a politically and socially embedded practice. As an urban-based phenomenon, fashion works to culturally subordinate rural societies. Perhaps it could also be used to reconnect rural, less Westernised forms of artistic production and display with urban youth. In short, the incredible cultural promise of African fashion needs to be exploited by a programme that is designed to address the disarticulation between cultural and economic autonomy.

NOTE

1.
The research in Dakar (1991-4) of Hudita Nura Mustafa was supported by grants from the Wenner-Gren Foundation for Anthropological Research, the Social Science Research Council Africa program and the American Council of Learned Societies.

Page 37
Fashion show, Dakar, Senegal, September 1992
Courtesy of Hudita Nura Mustafa

Page 46
Design by Xuly Bët, Bamako, Mali/Paris, France
Photo: Gauthier Gallet, Paris, France
Courtesy Cristofoli Press

Page 47
Design by Marian Fassler, Johannesburg,
South Africa
Courtesy Marian Fassler

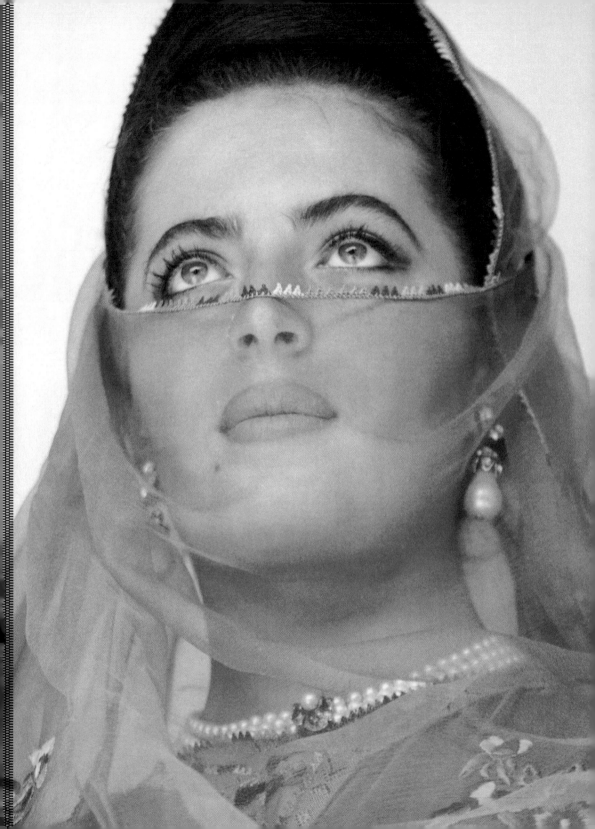

Covering the body in Africa: for what modernity?

MOUNIRA KHEMIR

Design by Zineb Joundy,
Casablanca, Morocco
Photo: Amar Abd Rabbo
Courtesy of Zineb Joundy

Next page
Agadez, Niger, 1975
Courtesy of the photographer:
Bernard Plossu, Paris, France

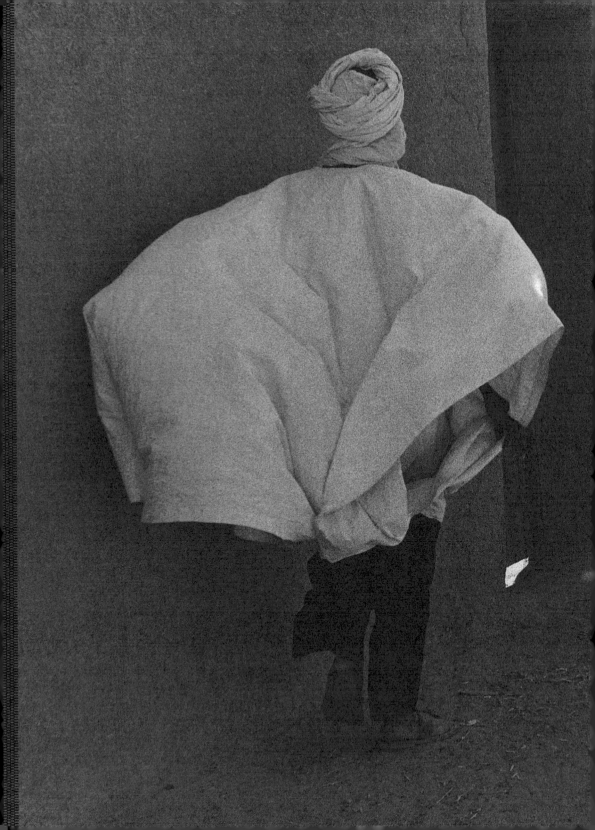

'It is, yet it is not / Water cannot wet it / Sabres cannot cut it' and 'A casket of saffron spread over the land / No sultan or bey can turn it to his hand', these are two popular Tunisian riddles which reflect the wealth of meaning contained in the two eternal paradigms of shadow and light, of what is hidden and what is revealed – in other words, the importance of suggestibility as the primary dimension of an aesthetic. While the veil, through its links with the Islamic world, appears in Western eyes to be replete with meaning, its significance extends beyond the notion of covering the female body and re-emerges in a number of extremely varied forms as an essential component of a culture. In architecture, the veil denotes an entire relationship to space, evoking secret and magical writings of all kinds, links with the sacred and the spiritual.

The other day my mother saw me leafing through the magazine Elle. My attention was caught by a photograph of a model whose hair was kept in place with hair clips. As I studied its intricate architecture, she suddenly exclaimed 'You know, Bedouin women used to do their hair just the same way – in fact they still do'. Taking the magazine from me, she added, 'Except they only cut the fringes at the sides, and their heads were covered.' Later I was to recall these women in their black, red or purple melias and brightly-coloured flowered neckerchiefs. Their names still fascinate me – names like Touffaha, Yacouta or Zmorda, scented like exotic fruits or glittering like rare precious stones.

In the countries of northwest Africa – part of the Islamic world – there is a logic of form which is not immediately accessible. Yet it conveys a basic truth: that of the human gaze which must be warded off, kept at a distance, a segregation of public and private life in which women must wear masks, the ultimate form of which is the Afghan chadari, inspired in turn by that basic feature of Arab-Islamic architecture, the moucharaby. Rather than a cultural or ethnic choice, these are artistic principles which recur throughout the Islamic world. However, covering the body calls for the construction of fictions in a world where the sexes were very strictly segregated and which seems bound to evolve in this age of major socio-economic transformation – an age which calls for a change in the status of women and hence a new relationship with the body.

Traditionally it was poets who enjoyed the privilege of singing the body's praises. The delights afforded by Arabic poetry – the qasida and the ghazal – are the private delights of the oasis, the secret garden. This is in fact a preoccupation with the human gaze which, with its emphasis on suggestibility, has caused a profound love of nuance to develop into an all-embracing courtesy which extends to the language and even appears in various popular expressions: thus a blind man may be referred to 'he who is called the seer' and a deaf man as 'he whose ear has a long antechamber'.

A new perfume launched in Paris this summer was named after a kind of green tea and the fresh colours of spring. This reminded me of the 'lords of the desert' – those mysteriously veiled men of blue and their fondness for the silvery leaves of green tea, which curl in upon themselves. The notion of covering immediately evokes that of the veil. However, the veil has taken many

It is, yet it is not
Water cannot wet it
Sabres cannot cut it

(Shadow)

A casket of saffron spread over the land No sultan or bey can turn it to his hand

(The sun)

different forms in the Arab-Islamic world. Moreover, it would be wrong to think that only women are veiled. There are also men, such as the Tuaregs, who wear robes or veils. A Tuareg would feel quite naked without his 'chèche', which he considers to be his most essential garment. The following story is alleged to be true. A man was washing at a water hole, stark naked, when to his horror a woman herding goats suddenly caught sight of him. He grabbed his breeches and used them to cover not his private parts, but his face! On reflection, I can see why. A faceless body could belong to anyone, whereas his blushing face would have been instantly identifiable.[1]

In any case, the days when the desert served purely as a backdrop for fashion photography are gone. For many years Africa, the desert, the Sahara simply meant places where film crews could go to record mirages, sand dunes and exotic scenery. But now, from one end of Africa to the other, we are witnessing the emergence of young designers whose variety of style has already gained them an international reputation.

In North Africa, women's clothing is a matter of outline. Yet the various sources (including miniatures) suggest that women's hairstyles have varied much more in response to changing fashions than other features of their apparel. They were often a mark of social rank. Women have been torn between their cultural heritage and a Western-inspired aesthetic. Although classic clothes were in fashion for many years, the modern style is more relaxed. Apart from clothing styles, American television series such as Dallas and Dynasty project all kinds of behavioural images. Some of today's skirts are considered too short for girls to wear and are forbidden at school. Smocks are compulsory for schoolgirls, although not for schoolboys. This is a question of custom rather than fashion, in which the ephemeral has different implications. There is a dividing line between everyday clothes and clothes worn on special occasions. At religious or family celebrations, both adults and children vie with one another for elegance. Fresh from the hairdresser's and decked out in smart clothes and new shoes, they parade up and down the streets. Asked what they think is the best brand of trainers or jeans, young people in various African countries would all agree, irrespective of cost – the main thing is to be in fashion. This is a far cry from the former relationship with clothing, whose colour and smell made them a kind of second skin. Nowadays, the second skin is a branded garment from the USA or France. Elegance and refinement are taking quite unexpected forms, although more traditional young women in Rabat or Bamako still go to their local dressmaker or tailor for the ultimate in smartness.

Traditional forms of the veil still exist, such as the haïk or the safsari, covering the entire body including the head, except for the two eyes or even just one, or just the lower half of the face, concealed by a veil. The Moroccan djellaba, a long hooded tunic in a variety of colours, used to be worn with a veil. Hence the care devoted to eye make-up. 'Al-Mokhala aux sept miroirs' – the seven-mirrored vial of kohl – indicates the importance attached to the human gaze and eye make-up, as reflected in various turns of phrase which convey multiple layers of meaning. People who want to say 'I haven't seen you for a long time, I've missed you' can use an Arabic phrase which, literally translated, means 'my eyes have not been darkened with kohl'. Even architecture conforms to the law that women must be segregated. As many nineteenth century travellers to the Orient noticed, women resemble veiled houses. Houses were previously surrounded by three antechambers to prevent eavesdropping; women spoke in low voices to safeguard their modesty. Sultan Mohammed V of Morocco caused a considerable shock in 1943 when he presented his daughter Aïcha to the nation without a veil.

Various pictorial and written sources reveal that, even though women never left the home unveiled, they were familiar with the tricks of fashion that enabled them to make subtle changes to their appearance. Yet in Western depictions of Oriental women, whether by orientalist painters or by photographers, the women are either simply veiled or unveiled, exoticised or de-exoticised. A good example is the famous painting by Delacroix entitled 'Femmes d'Alger dans leur appartement' (women of Algiers in their quarters). When Picasso took up the same theme, the women were stripped naked and the space was opened up. This highly revealing Western approach to the Oriental world can be traced throughout the course of art history.

To stylists such as Azzedine Alaïa, women must remain inaccessible. Rather than the veil, it is the symbol behind it that he sees as the essence of Oriental womanhood. Although he designs women's dresses so close-fitting that they become a kind of ornamentation, a second skin, Alaïa has by no means renounced his origins. Given his reputation as a keen user of new materials, particularly stretch fabrics, he would seem at first sight to be anti-traditional – and yet, behind this outright modernity, one can sometimes glimpse another profile which links him to his native culture. His aim is to design erotic women's clothes which arouse desire. This is an interactive image of woman and an aesthetic which inevitably conjures up the terms of a 'relational' aesthetic. Things in the Oriental world are reflected not in mirrors, but in other people's eyes – hence the great importance of social bonds. The human gaze is fascinating and sinful by turns. At the heart of desire is the human gaze, which is perceived differently from one culture to another.

There are dress codes and conventions, but today young people throughout the world – including Africa – are deflecting the symbols of social conformity. The rhythmic chanting of rap musicians is now symbolised by loose clothing – a fashion which at first appeared to be the antithesis of fashion. Here the sources of inspiration are manifold, with interpretations ranging from cyberspace to mediaeval and tribal custom and back again. Today, from Africa to China, young people wear Titanic or Spice Girls T-shirts – symbols of the cool nineties, which are also taking over Africa. Yet, as Africa discovers Europe, Europe is proving hungrier for novelty than any other continent, in a process of rediscovery, creation and deflection. It is now up to Africa to rediscover its own treasures, buried between form and matter, as it explores the paths of fashion. From one end of Africa to the other, the modern age is not so much a matter of unchanged authenticity as a new way – or ways – of seeing things without forgetting one's origins. Clothing may become the extension of a yearned-for life or change of space.

Like the topography of space, a labyrinth waiting to be explored, as worn by betrothed young girls from desert tribes buried under as many as seven layers of clothing or by young married women from Casablanca, Morocco or Hammamet, Tunisia, the veil is always there to celebrate some rite of initiation. The present-day costume for the jelwa (unveiling of the bride), known as el-kiswa el-kbira, is one of the richest in Tunisia. There are three superimposed garments, invisible beneath the gilded tunic. In certain tales, the mirror as we know it appears to be virtually unknown. An old man tells the story of a woman who, after quarrelling with her husband one day, left home and went to visit her daughters, on each of whom she played a trick. She told the eldest: 'Daughter, your husband has another woman. His face appeared to me as I leaned over the oil jar. Daughter, take heed, he has another woman.' The daughter instantly ran to the jar and saw the reflection of her own face. She smashed the jar to get at her rival, and oil poured all over the floor. Even more than the daughter's gullibility, in the context that concerns us this story conveys the notion almost of an anti-mirror or a magic mirror.

In the 1970s, during a summer in which there were many celebrations, my grandmother said she thought women's backs were too bare. Yet their backs were not accessible to everyone. At celebrations the women and men are usually segregated. The women would come in wearing their silk safsaris (their rank indicated by the quality of the silk in their veils). They were adorned with gold jewellery, and some of the older ones wore heavy anklets, but the most astonishing thing was their perfume, Rêve d'Or, which was in fashion at the time and did not fail to stir the nostrils of the men, seated in rows outside the house. This heady perfume was the women's sole response to the men's gaze. They had chosen to drench themselves in it as their only form of veil. The love of perfume which has prevailed in the Orient since time immemorial has become proverbial in the West. A perfume seller in the souks of Tunis will tell you that amber is just the thing for winter evenings and that jasmine goes perfectly with the scents of spring. This subtle vision forms the basis for an entire aesthetic which now survives only in prose.

The veil is the expression and aesthetic dimension of an entire way of speaking at a time of great social change, and hence of new relationships to the body and the inevitable emergence of new ways of talking about it. It is not a question of evoking or conjuring up a bygone world, but rather of attempting wherever possible to capture images of a living world, far from the myth of crystalline clarity and ineffable transparency – a world of segregation between that which is without and that which is within.

What inner essence is preserved, and what form of elegance sought, when the body is covered? The veil never serves just one single purpose. It may also be used to cover furniture, as is done at times of mourning in the countries of northwest Africa. Although the connotations associated with the veil make it seem almost like a fabric of the devil, its recurrence in so many different situations gives it an essential dimension in this culture. When going to offer their condolences to the family of someone who had died, women from the town of Sfax, Tunisia used to drape a

zerzhana[2] over their usual tunic – a woollen jebba in winter and a silk one in summer, worn inside out as a sign of mourning. The veil, as a mark of detachment from the tangible world, may avail itself of the muteness of the pattern to play out endless variations on a theme.

It is also an expression of the capabilities of these men and women of the desert. Here, aesthetics are not divorced from ethics. In Africa, as elsewhere, weaving is one of the earliest expressions of human endeavour, with various interpretations throughout the continent. In fact, 'expression' and 'speech' are the words one is tempted to use when referring to it. Indeed, in the Dogon language, the same word is used for 'speech' and 'fabric'.[3] It is possible to imagine, when touching the colour indigo, that a fabric can have all the depth of a narrative.

Access to images from different cultures will inevitably allow new ethnic symbols to circulate and hence to be recombined. Certain stylists, such as Alphadi (Niger), use writing, signs and symbols – a highly original concept, like that of Katoucha (Guinea/London), whose designs impregnate the wearer's hands and legs as an extension of the pattern of the fabric.[4] The body will be covered and loose garments worn in a link with spirituality. Authenticity will no longer mean what it used to, but will be blended and deflected, just as it always has been in music.

Today, the world of fashion cannot afford to disregard new rhythms, new ways of listening to the world, perhaps a new synthesis between brand-new and worn apparel. As this century draws to a close, all these new materials may be leading us towards the essential spirit of material. Sombre or faded colours call for a different type of search – a search for a form of spirituality which will show that true riches lie within ourselves. Like other art forms, fashion is in search of a new field of endeavour, that of spirituality. In these African cultures, adorning oneself is an act which involves not only the whole body, but also the soul. It is not, as so often in Europe, an act of narcissism. Perhaps we will soon be seeing the garment-as-talisman, the magical garment which was invented in the Islamic and African worlds by the masters of the human gaze, almost as a means of protection. Like all art forms, ornaments, garments and veils have links with both the sacred and the profane. They give individuals a place in time and help them to forge their identities.

Design by Zineb Joundy,
Casablanca, Morocco
Photo: Amar Abd Rabbo
Courtesy of Zineb Joundy

NOTES

1.

Bernezat, Odette; *Hommes des montagnes du Hoggar*, Editions des 4 seigneurs, Grenoble, 1975, p. 177

2.

Les costumes traditionnels féminins de Tunisie, Collectif, Maison tunisienne de l'édition, Tunis, 1978

3.

Fauque, Claude and Otto Wollenweber; *Tissus d'Afrique*, Syros Alternatives, Paris, 1991, p. 37

4.

Revue Noire, special issue on fashion, December 1997-January-February 1998

Woman, Tunisia, 1995
© of the photographer:
Joss Dray, Paris, France

Street-scene, Tunisia, 1995
© of the photographer:
Joss Dray, Paris, France

Hair design by Roger Amangoua
at the Festival Mondial, Cannes,
France, 1998, model: Stéphanie
Courtesy of Amina, Paris, France

Hair statements in urban Africa: the Beauty, the Mystic and the Madman

T.K. BIAYA

Page 80
The wigmaker, Mali, 1995
Courtesy of the photographer: Peter Bettenhausen, Museon, The Hague, the Netherlands

Dakar, Senegal, 1998
Courtesy of T.K. Biaya

A visit to major black urban communities in Africa and elsewhere reveals a striking phenomenon: beyond the three social categories symbolised by the Beauty, the Mystic and the Madman (recognisable by their meticulously styled hair, their long braids or tresses, and their shaved heads or unruly mops respectively), the observant visitor will be fascinated by both the uniformity and the variety of hair and hairstyles, and indeed of the clothes worn by both males and females (adults, young people and children). The proliferation of hairdressing salons and fashion houses and the accompanying advertisements is evidence of this culture of beauty and elegance, which is not unrelated to globalisation. In this world of global markets, of commercialisation and consumption of practices, this culture of beauty is evolving out of local knowledge, technique and meaning which are now being blended by the international media, transnational migration and the transplantation of African national communities to other parts of Africa and the West. These voyages, which are more often individual than collective, have ultimately created an economic and cultural space for the immigrants concerned and promoted an African identity based on know-how relating to the treatment of hair. Under the impact of cultural globalisation, these designs will follow two paths: on the one hand, hairdressing salons will internationalise hairstyles (which have become basic necessities), and on the other they will trigger off a reaction in the form of local designs, rebelliously clinging to the economic logic of the marketplace.

The form and practice of this age-old art involve a process of disintegration and integration, as African designs are taken to the West to form hybrids which are more likely to spread in Western rather than African cities. To assess this social phenomenon, it is interesting to analyse its form, then the factors involved in its development, and finally its current status in a globalising world.

HAIR IN URBAN CULTURE: A FORM WHICH LINKS ETHNOGRAPHY AND FASHION

In present-day Africa, hair and its treatment have escaped from the context of mere domestic practice, devoid of political meaning except insofar as recorded in ethnographic literature or exhibited in museums. Hairdressing fashions, beauty competitions and fashion shows have led to the emergence of a falsely homogeneous world in which hair remains part of the dominant ideology of beauty based on the Western aesthetic tradition[1] – a tradition which has never been challenged by the various social, political and cultural protest movements, despite their borrowings from various world cultures. Nevertheless, hair has ultimately acquired a degree of political meaning of its own, which it transmits to the local and international community as part of its cultural identity or expression. Based on the sampling and mixing techniques of American rap music[2], this model, and successive hair and hairdressing fashions, are an expression of protest and cultural practice rather than of beauty as such. The attempt by Africa's political elite to express an intrinsically African identity through traditional hairstyles and braiding has failed to convert young people to this substitute nationalistic ideology. Yet this rejection provides a new avenue for the emergence of an urban youth culture which is spreading (at least in people's imagination, even if resources are lacking) thanks to the creative and also subversive adoption of Western practices. I shall return to this later. Young Africans have associated hairstyle with a vitality which can be overtly expressed by what their hair says to the people around them, in a context where the intertextuality and multiplicity of languages sometimes fill the gap and make the required statement. Such forms warrant a more detailed study, in which leading proponents of a particular art form and their unconventional hairstyles – Bob Marley and reggae, BIG, Tupac Shakur and rap, Dennis Rodman and basketball, Mike Tyson and boxing – both subjugate and symbolise an African identity and an art form in which violence is the key to contemporary success and which point the way for male and female identity in Africa. Moreover, these decontextualised borrowings link young Africans to the rest of the world, of which they feel they are an integral part. Without wishing to describe in further detail the process by which this new identity is emerging[3], there is one major phenomenon which runs counter to African culture: the social meaning of braids – still an essentially feminine feature in Africa – has been distorted now that young men have started wearing them as a symbol of masculinity. This eccentric appropriation of feminine features by men has led to a confused situation which has been referred to as 'gender jamming'. This wearing of braids conveys a false sense of sexual equality, since it helps the male-dominated American rap culture to triumph in Africa, where 'Bad Sistas' are few in number and are seldom heard. The politics of gender and competition between American and African culture must also be considered in the context of this hybridity, which continues to appeal to the young.

Behind these emerging forms, B. Jewsiewicki[4] has pointed out that the history of African old styles of hair and hairstyling[5], which is still caught in the straitjacket of ethnography and exoticism, not to mention fashion, is outlining an African aesthetic which extends beyond symbolic, heterological research[6] and missionary research into meaning. This aesthetic underwent significant changes with the emergence of modern urban culture from the beginning of the twentieth century onwards. The hair and hairdressing practices current in the largely Portuguese trading centres along the coast of Africa (such as St. Louis, Ouidah, San Salvador and Luanda), which grew up from the end of the fifteenth century onwards and/or were involved in the slave trade, followed a path of their own which differed from that in colonial towns and cities. The slave-trading towns had a system of 'pigmentocracy' which was also found in the West Indies[7] and was reflected in the social status and hairstyles of the 'signares'. These slave traders' companions were half-caste women, superior in social rank to other natives and forbidden to surrender to African aesthetics by braiding their hair as ordinary native women did. Their lofty hairstyles and richly ornamented clothes were mainly intended to be shown off on balconies. They were there to alleviate the expatriates' brooding fantasies and feelings of homesickness rather than to satisfy their sensual needs – a sort of tropical version of the courtesans they had left back home in Europe. In revenge, the colonial cities, founded as bastions of 'civilisation', rapidly promoted the present-day African concept of beauty within the same Western-oriented aesthetic 'épistèmé'.

Colonised Africans set about the laborious task of straightening their curly hair and wearing European hairstyles in keeping with prevailing city fashions. Scarification, tattooing and traditional hairstyles, now considered out-of-date and backward, rapidly disappeared between 1910 and 1935[8] and gave way to a contrary trend. This effort to transform African hair and skin was pursued by the new political middle class and leisured elite in the years after independence. In his psychological portrait of colonised man, Frantz Fanon declared that his processes of mimicry included a desire to sleep with a white woman, skin-lightening and a whole set of hair-related attitudes and behaviours (hair-straightening and partings) as well as certain linguistic attitudes. Yet reality is not so simple, for in the midst of this deracialising process Africans were also developing a tactical creative ability based on a need to resist their oppressors by such means as 'négritude', Pan-Africanism, the independence movement, the 'black is beautiful' ideology, Afro hairstyles and so on.

Alongside this intellectual resistance movement there was also a popular movement. Ironically, it was this movement that was to usher in cultural change, for it was the generator of local urban culture. Bars, football matches, Christian and Islamic religious festivals, traditional wrestling matches and concerts rapidly became centres where men and women could boldly affirm their need to be seen through clothing fashions and modern body care, and hairstyling was considered the crowning glory of elegance. In the case of women, this cult of beauty drew on a number of different sources and compelled hair-braiders, weavers and hairdressers, who were no longer bound by socialising practices and parochial ethnic constraints, to become more professional. For men, it meant the irreversible adoption of Western models.

CHANGING PRACTICES IN CENTRAL AFRICA; A SHORT HISTORY

The first pictures and imagery of popular songs of urban Central Africa (including such cities as Kinshasa, Brazzaville, Douala and Libreville) reveal little variety in hairstyles, nor do they give any indication that women or men pay particular attention to their hair, with the exception of the Mangbetu with his cockerel on his shoulder.9 In these male-dominated, essentially working-class cities, in the years after the Second World War, men gradually became acquainted with Western-style hair care, while women modernised through dance music. They dressed quickly in the West African style, wearing a kita and a libaya (top) with a matching kitambala (neckerchief). Women either concealed their hair in headscarves or else shaved their heads and left them uncovered, whereas men made use of hair creams and other modern hairdressing techniques. The well-dressed man wore a suit and tie with a matching hat. In this way, with help from magazines, men's and women's fashion gradually developed and underwent the changes that were affecting the world and beauty products in general. Central Africa, where the art of hair-braiding was at its most highly developed, began experimenting with wire-braiding, a practice known in French as 'antennes', or 'radio aerials'. This name was significant because it conjured up images of the woman announcer on Radio Stanleyville (now Kisangani) and of the singer Lucie Eyenga – two

Hair design by Roger Amangoua
at the Festival Mondial, Cannes,
France, 1998
Courtesy of Amina, Paris, France

Hair design 'Gouye-gi' or Baobab
by Véronique Médor, Dakar, Senegal, 1998
Courtesy of Véronique Médor

women from the land of the Congo who personified beauty and successful urban womanhood. In such recently Christianised societies, the term was also suggestive of sexual enticement. After all, unmarried women succeeded by making themselves beautiful for unfaithful husbands or unmarried workers, who made them gifts of jewellery, pagnes (African-style wrap-skirts) and clothing accessories which they had earned by the sweat of their brow. In the context of nineteenth-century colonial society, male-female relations and faithfulness or unfaithfulness could also be read in the way that headscarves were worn by married and unmarried women. Unmarried women wore them elegantly knotted on top of their heads, in Senegalese or Sawa fashion, while married women wore them carelessly so as not to be too conspicuous. Subsequently it was only married women who were allowed to wear headscarves; unmarried women first had their hair curled with hot combs, and later treated with a soda-based hair-straightener known as zazou or else with hair-stiffening agents which were imported from Zambia and Nigeria from 1960 onwards.

Headscarves provided a truly paradigmatic division between traditional and modern hair care. In uncovering and wire-braiding their hair, Central African women were moving away from older concepts of beauty and at the same time rejecting forms of body decoration (such as tattooing, scarification and tooth-filing) which had served to mark the transition from childhood to puberty and adulthood. The new regional fashion of wire-braiding was later to make way for wigs, whose success went hand in hand with 'xessal' or 'ambi' (skin-lightening). The global harmonisation of clothing through fashion shows, the promotion of pagnes and the emergence of national beauty contests was counterbalanced by local hair fashions, which were enriched by the input, through exchanges between countries, of the hairdressing know-how and techniques generated by such contests.

Unlike in the usa, where the wearing of Afro hairstyles or Black Panther berets was an affirmation of Afro-American political identity in response to white domination, there was no hair-related identity policy in Africa until President Mobutu introduced his authenticity policy in 1971, at a time when Lumumba-style partings were all the rage in Dakar and other urban African communities. The concept of authenticity now produced a rift in this regional bloc. Trousers, wigs, mini-skirts or mini-dresses and skin-lightening were now prohibited in what was then called Zaire and became restricted to other parts of Central Africa. Attractive Zairean women no longer imitated Western models; their modern ornaments made way for cowries and other shells or vegetable products which they used to decorate their braided hair, in keeping with the boldness of their pagnes. Men, no longer allowed to wear suits and ties, switched to the abacos, a Mao-style suit with a cravat in place of a tie. Mobutu's wife Marie-Antoinette appeared in public with braided hair, alongside her abacos-suited husband. This policy brought hair-braiding, a practice which had originated in the Sudanese and Bantu cultures of the northwestern forest region, back to the fore. As this age-old art was reinstated, various blends of ancient and modern began to emerge. This exhausting, intricate practice, which often required the wearer to remain motionless for hours at a

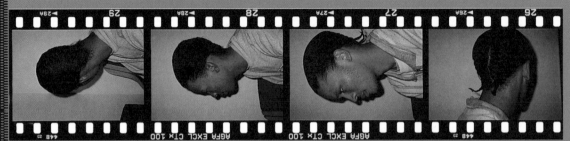
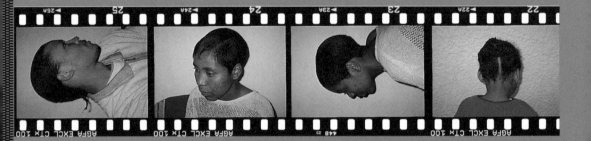

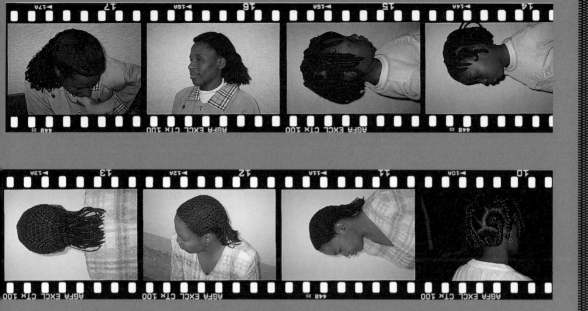

Hair designs in Gaborone, Botswana, 1998
Photos: Nini van Driel, Amsterdam,
the Netherlands

stretch, was the forerunner of today's hairdressing salons. This 'suki ya maboko' hairstyle was dubbed 'African beauty' and 'bakutu' or 'omanga' after popular female singers.

The authenticity policy, launched at a time of relative prosperity, encouraged trade in pagnes and its two daughters: fashion and hairstyling. The natural-hair wigs which, thanks to modern technology, now flooded into the country were in keeping with the new focus on pagnes; in Central Africa this opened up the gates to West African designs, which henceforth took precedence over local ones. Despite the economic crisis in the years after 1980, the influx of cosmetics and hairstyles (including hairpieces and the different styles which they made possible), as well as the skills which were needed to handle them, was to lead to the emergence of hairdressing salons in the wake of fashion houses.

AFRICAN HAIRDRESSING SALONS

Except in religious or therapeutic settings, hairdressing was a means of socialisation for women and girls, who chatted to each other as their hair was being done, and became the exclusive preserve of 'griottes' and hair-braiders, who in traditional society were responsible for dressing the hair of athletes, nobility and royalty. With the modernisation of Africa and an increasing demand for good-quality work, this function has evolved into a specialised profession. Professional schools of hairdressing with curricula including modern hairstyling, hair-braiding, unisex styling, headscarves, pedicure, manicuring, massage and make-up, as well as biology, anatomy and physiology, have sprung up rapidly in such cities as Dakar, Abidjan and Kinshasa. These curricula are, of course, based on those of the European schools from which managers and owners of hairdressing salons have graduated. These salons and schools have taken ancient forms and patterns of hair-braiding and hairstyling and imbued them with new meaning, at the same time becoming a focus for inspiration and new design. However, the survival and success of hairdressing salons depend not so much on their mastery of hairdressing skills as on their ability to help their customers be seen within their society or social group, according to the rank which they hold within it. At the same time, the international trade in hairpieces which has recently taken Africa by storm has linked up the continent to America and Europe, introducing hairstyles, techniques and products which had previously only been seen on television and in magazines. This technological input and the imaginative potential of the new prefabricated hairstyles (including wigs in various shades of colour) have allowed new combinations of hairstyling, clothing and make-up in conjunction with local practices. Following on from 'Maracas d'Or', the 'Nattes 1998' competition between Cameroon's top ten hairdressing salons (organised by Nina et Mimi, a company which sells hairpieces) has shown not only how creative these local firms are, but also how deeply they are involved in the globalisation process by turning braids into a basic necessity. Hairdressing has now joined the range of products on the African market which are exclusively feminine (even if ultimately intended to fulfil the expectations of a male-dominated society), namely pagnes, cosmetics, beauty contests and fashion shows.

Hair design 'Djagné', modern creation
by Salon Ramses, Pout, Senegal, 1998,
model: Fatou Mbaye
Courtesy of Amina, Paris, France

Hair design by Roger Amangoua
at the Festival Mondial, Cannes,
France, 1998, model: Fabienne
Courtesy of Amina, Paris, France

DIFFERENT STYLES IN URBAN WEST AFRICA

While differing economic conditions certainly influence the way in which beauty care develops in different cities, they do not prevent innovation from breaking through everywhere. Abidjan and Bamako project two contrasting images. While Abidjan, a miniature Manhattan, is bursting with economic vigour and modern leisure facilities, Bamako, despite its limited resources, has the strength derived from a healthy culture in which old and new features are cheerfully combined, highlighting its glorious past and rationalising its values. For all their rich variety of braiding, hairstyles in Bamako are discreet, in keeping with the available resources and the sobriety of local women, whose pagnes and bogolan (a locally dyed fabric) are nevertheless in demand in Dakar and Abidjan. This culture of beauty and the wearing of long, uncovered, natural hair contrasts sharply with the situation in Abidjan, with its dyed and boldly dressed and braided hairstyles, so reminiscent of the West with their avant-garde look. The styling of hairpieces is so rich and varied that it is easy to forget that this intricate work – which necessitates keeping still for up to two days and often gives the wearer a headache – originated in Wolof country, where the braiders are recruited. The Wolof style of hair-braiding, which these artists from Senegal or elsewhere nowadays combine with styles 'sampled' from other ethnic groups such as the Peuls or the Toucouleurs, first appeared around 1920. It can be found in 'Dakar Village' neighbourhood in Brazzaville and in the name given to a way of wearing headscarves in Kinshasa. What has helped to make Senegalese hairstyling paramount is the arrival in Abidjan of Senegalese fashion models who, with their extra height and delicate features, have ousted local models. Senegalese hair-braiders have been welcomed with open arms, first by local fashion houses and later by local hairdressing salons. Their reputation has even preceded them to the United States, where they are in great demand in Afro-American salons. Their names and designs now appear in black fashion magazines and advertising catalogues.

'HEADDRESS' AS A FORM OF YOUTH PROTEST

Today it is common to hear French-speaking Africans using the word 'coiffe' (headdress). This new usage, which comes from a misread sign on the window of a Congolese hairdresser in Paris, refers to any hairstyle that differs from the conventional hairstyles worn by people who are out of touch with the latest fashion. This cultural authentication of a misinterpreted term goes to show just how much power it conveys in the world of young people who are at odds with their own society and want to keep in touch with today's globalising world. Young people in African cities have borrowed two Afro-American hairstyles and developed them into global hairstyles imbued with a special local meaning, in which 'headdress' has become a vector of protest. Once invested with this social power, which conveys the notion of protest in its historic context, such hairstyles, having become utterable, enable young people to be seen in a society in the throes of crisis, by allowing them to make a social or political statement through the productive activity in which they themselves are engaging. This surrogate violence is often a response to the structural violence inherent in African cities, where unemployment, economic crisis and the collapse of tribal solidarity have gone hand in hand with neglect and violence on the part of the state.

Both of these hairstyles are short. In the first, the hair is bleached or dyed yellow and cut to the same length all over the head. In the second, the hair is cut short at the front, with three parallel partings, and the rest of the head is shaved. There is also a blend of the two styles, with short hair all over the head and a bleached tuft at the front.

'LA COIFFE JOSPIN' IN KINSHASA

The musician Defao Matumona, from Congo-Brazzaville, a well-known sapeur in both Africa and the West, dubbed the first of the two hairstyles 'la coiffe Jospin', after the current French prime minister. This was a reference to the fighting spirit displayed by Lionel Jospin during a TV debate with his opponent in the 1994 presidential elections, Jacques Chirac. In adopting this name and hairstyle, young people were expressing their opposition to the crisis-ridden Mobutu dictatorship and its obstruction of attempts to introduce democracy. 'La coiffe Jospin' rapidly spread within musicians' circles and among young people who sought change and wanted to be seen.

THE BIRTH OF ASANTE

Historians of African clothing and hairstyle have noted that, except in Nigeria and Ghana, local clothing and hairstyles have been abandoned in favour of Western fashions throughout English-speaking Africa.[10] Without necessarily suggesting a causal link between indirect rule and the promotion of local clothing and hairstyles, it is a striking fact they have only been retained by societies which have not altered their ancient ways of life in the modern age (such as the Masai and the Ndebele). In French-speaking Central and West Africa, on the other hand, African beauticians have vigorously continued to create new hair designs. Here, African designs and influences are more prominent than non-African ones, and artistic creations borrow elements from one another as they circulate from country to country. Admittedly, this endogenous cultural dynamism depends on inter-African trade in pagnes, with Lomé emerging as the capital of imported textiles – Dutch wax and java (both Dutch designed and produced textiles) while Dakar and Kinshasa continue to monopolise stylistic design and Abidjan acts as an entrepreneur and cultural broker, promoting and redistributing women's products in Africa and throughout the world.

This post-colonial division of labour in the promotion of clothing and hairstyle has had very little impact on Ghana and Nigeria which, taking advantage of their age-old tradition in this area, have instead generated a vast market among the Afro-American diaspora and in the West Indies rather than in Africa itself. This cultural process, which is symbolised by the word Asante ('the unbroken circle', derived from Ashanti), began with the black revival and the wearing of the various forms of kente, from headdresses to elegant suits of clothes and even badges symbolising

Hair design 'Mbada' by Salon
Ndoyenne, Dakar, Senegal, 1997
Courtesy of Amina, Paris, France

Benedict McCarthy with players of Bafana Bafana, South Africa

Courtesy of Andrew Lanning, Touchline Photo, Cape Town, South Africa

the reunion between the child (the diaspora) and the mother continent of Africa, and eventually also extended to hair design. Not only are these creations, including those of hairdressers and hair designers, exhibited at Afro-American celebrations such as Kwanzaa, New Year and weddings, but they also reflect the Africanisation of American black culture and the constant presence of an African identity within the American cultural mainstream, through the work of art photographers such as Ephrem Hunte, the braided hairstyles of rappers and young people.

DENNIS RODMAN AND BAFANA BAFANA

More than his talent as a sportsman, it is his eccentricity, brutal violence, hostile manner and antisocial escapades which have made Dennis Rodman of the Chicago Bulls so popular among young Africans. In the context of South Africa, where violence shows no sign of abating and Afro-Americans are the role models for young blacks, Rodman's behaviour is imitated not only by the members of the South African soccer team, Bafana Bafana, but also by young people in street gangs. In a bar in the Johannesburg suburb of Hillbrow, just after we had heard gunshots on the evening that the South African team were returning home, a young man called Ishaak had no hesitation in asserting that this ever-colourful figure was a symbol of protest against a system of values ranging from apartheid to the lack of understanding which young people faced at home. He saw the players' unruly behaviour as part of this model, and in this connection remarked on the attitudes and the bleached hair of soccer player Benedict McCarthy and the teenage boys and girls around us.

MIKE TYSON AND THE 'BOUL FALÉ'

In 1997, the catchphrase 'boul falé' (be or stay cool) spread like wildfire in Dakar, in response to the aggressive rivalry between two wrestlers representing different wards of the city, symbolising the division between newcomers to Dakar (known as 'kao kao') and long-time residents, and thus stirring up the passions of the wrestlers and their fans. The fight was won by Mohamed Ndao alias Tyson, who was proclaimed a 'boul falé'. Following his victory, his hairstyle (which resembles that of the American boxer Mike Tyson) has become the hallmark of the young generation. The catchphrase has come to symbolise a break with traditional Wolof family ideals and values (marriage, solidarity, sharing and seniority) and a withdrawal from national politics. Instead, young people are free to dream of going to America, of becoming Modou Modou (international Mouride traders; mouridism is the Islam of Senegal) and of taking up sport as a prelude to moving abroad. Wrestlers wear this second hairstyle in combination with the American flag, which they wrap around themselves while dancing just before fights. In everyday life, young 'boul falé' wear T-shirts portraying the shaved heads of two proponents of American rap and violence, Tupac Shakur and BIG, both of them now dead.

CONCLUSION: THE PARADOXES OF GLOBAL HYBRIDITY, THE SELF AND A DIVINE ART FORM

Today, hair continues to be more than a mere basic essential. Although it has lost much of the traditional pomp and prestige which made it a locus for the expression of divinity or virility or for change in society, it has nonetheless managed, in a globalising world, to negotiate a space in which its native culture has become established. Hair has turned into a locus of memory. Similarly, in this refusal to surrender, dreadlocks are still seen as an expression of Mouride mysticism, while paradoxically they are trivialised by the Rastafarian, another 'Mystic' weeping for his lost paradise. Yet the identity conveyed by this hairstyle goes beyond both the individual and collective selves, and points to a twofold orientation in the search for identity: the hybridity of a millennial art form which, having become a basic essential, seeks to perfect itself by absorbing new techniques and the products of new technology in this global village where there is less and less investigation of origins. In return, the voyages made by the techniques and motifs – or rather, the vanishing ancient symbols – which Mimi or Odette have taken with them from Congo to Hillbrow in South Africa or from Chad to Lefrak City in Queens, New York, are not only an illustration of the unexpected transnational voyages made by both beauticians and the Mangbetu-style walo walo braids which they discovered in Lubumbashi or Abidjan and are now combining with hairpieces or synthetic plants produced in the USA, but they also go to make up the art form which Laurence K. so vainly sought on arriving from London. At the same time, Afro-American women have decontextualised African hairstyles and their meaning and subsequently given them an admixture of creativity and black culture politics. This has resulted in beautiful, bold designs[11] in which input from other cultures has wrought transformations and changes unsuspected even by Khady-Rasta when she transferred her know-how from Sicap rue 10 in Dakar to New York.

Moreover, African hairdressing has now assimilated technology and has thrust its cultural practices upon the world, not as a museum-type exhibit, but as a form of beauty and a means of expressing or narrating the fractured or ailing selves of African (or indeed global) youth in search of identity and protest, in this postmodern world where media overkill has tended to reduce cultural hair and hairdressing practices to African practices spiced up with a dash of Afro-American culture. All that remains of the ethnic identity of African hairstyling is the technique, the Way; yet surely, as former President of Senegal and poet Léopold Senghor said, art belongs to no single country. However, as long as our contemporary dinosaurs continue to exist, manatees (sea-cows) will continue to drink at the springs of the Masai and the Ndebele. And, in nostalgic mood, let us not forget that magical moment when, on the eve of a tabaski, the mistress of the house deigns to braid and dress her maid's hair. This striking tableau fleetingly conjures up a perfect dream of innocence in which distinctions of class and caste can be broken down by the dressing of hair.

NOTES

1.

Mercer, K.; *Welcome to the Jungle*, New Positions in Cultural Studies, Routledge, New York, London, 1994

2.

Rose, T., *Black Noise Rap Music and Black Culture in Contemporary America*, Wesleyan University Press, Hanover & London, 1994

3.

Biaya, T.K.; *Les paradoxes de la masculinité africaine moderne: une histoire de violences, d'immigration et de crises*, in: Canadian Folklore, 19,1: 99-112, 1997

4.

Jewsiewicki, B.; *De l'art africain et de l'esthétique, valeur d'usage, valeur d'échange*, in: Cahiers d'études africaines, 141-142, XXXVI, 1-2 : 257-269, 1996.

5.

Sagay, E.; *African Hair Style*, Heinemann, London, 1983

6.

Roberts, N. P. and A.F. Roberts (eds.); *Memory, Luba Art and the Making of History*, Prestel – Museum for African Art, Munich/New York, 1996

7.

Henriques, F.; *Family and Colour in Jamaica*, Secker & Warburg, London, 1953

8.

Diop, C. A.; *Antériorité des civilisations nègres: mythe ou vérité historique?* Présence africaine, Paris, 1967

9.

Biaya, T. K.; *Mundele, ndumba et ambiance. Le vrai bal blanc et noir. Aux sources de la sociabilité urbaine zaïroise*, in: G. de Villers (ed.), Belgique/Zaïre: quel avenir? Actes du colloque, Cahiers africains, 1994

10.

This became apparent in the wake of the recent tragic events in Kenya and Tanzania. In CNN pictures from the cemetery in Nairobi, the relatives of the dead were all wearing Western clothes.

11.

Evans, N.; *Everything You Need to Know About Hairlocking, Dread, African & Nubian Locks*, A & B Publishers Group, Brooklyn, New York, 1996.

Page 97

At the election of Miss Cascas,

Cascas, Senegal, 1998

Courtesy of PAOPIM/KIT, Dakar, Senegal/

Amsterdam, the Netherlands

Hair design by Roger Amangoua at the Festival

Mondial, Cannes, France, 1998, model: Nathalie

Courtesy of Amina, Paris, France

Page 100/101

Hairdresser's, Bamako, Mali, 1995

Courtesy of the photographer: Peter Bettenhausen,

Museon, The Hague, the Netherlands

Hairdresser's, Bamako, Mali, 1995
Courtesy of Peter Bettenhausen, Museon,
The Hague, the Netherlands

Peul styled by Alphadi at the
African Mosaïque Show,
© Ethiopean Children's Fund,
Addis Ababa, Ethiopia/New York, USA

Henna Mania: body painting as a fashion statement, from tradition to Madonna

SALAH M. HASSAN

Encountering familiar scenes in unfamiliar places often evokes pleasant memories, but it can also generate a feeling of unease and resentment. This is all the more true when the familiar is actually an intimate part of one's personal history and identity, and part of an esoteric culture one has grown into and known from the inside out. It is with more than a few mixed feelings, therefore, that I observe the current craze for henna body painting and note the differences – and similarities – with the kind of decorations I remember from my own native landscape, in Sudan. I recall the first time I entered a branch of the Body Shop, the well-known specialty chain which markets the kind of skin care products used for centuries by indigenous communities of Africa, Asia, Native Americas, Australia, and Oceania. I distinctly remember both excitement and resentment, if not outright anger, about what I characterise as an act of capitalist appropriation marketed as a nature-friendly and environmentally-safe enterprise.

For centuries, henna art has been part of the semiotics of daily life in the world I hail from. As a Sudanese, I grew up seeing its intricate designs on many of the women around me. It is an art practised by mothers, aunts, sisters, and on some occasions by a professional, a woman known as al hannana. A predominantly feminine art, henna painting was one of the keys by which we learned to identify the social, ritual or marital status of a woman. Henna designs and their placement on the body also distinguished the married from the unmarried or the virgin (or so it was claimed) and the circumcised from the uncircumcised. In other words, henna decorations function as a marker of social, ritual or marital status. Of course for such signification to work, it requires other variables such as hairstyle, jewellery, costume, make-up, and perfume. Henna is, therefore, part of an entire aesthetic system that includes the olfactory and tactile as necessary elements. Henna body art, as Aida Kanafani eloquently remarks, 'is symbolic of a value system and cultural pattern which ritualise the experiences of these senses.'[1]

SUDDENLY HENNA!

Browsing the shelves of a bookstore one recent summer afternoon, in the small town where I now live in upstate New York, I came across a book entitled 'Mehndi: The Timeless Art of Henna Painting'. Next to it, a sign promoting a book signing by the author, Loretta Roome, accompanied, as the sign announced, by 'two world renowned artists who will demonstrate the art of Mehndi.' The author's name sounded familiar, and I recalled an article which one of my students handed to me after a lecture on body art in Africa, torn from the pages of People magazine. In the article, Roome was photographed in a pose that evoked the image of Kali, the Indian goddess, with six hands outstretched and the palms decorated in intricate henna designs.

Neither Roome's book, nor the performance which accompanied its signing, should come as a surprise. Henna body painting, or Mehndi, as it is known in India, has become the latest craze among many of the icons of Western pop culture. Photo spreads in popular magazines feature super models and pop stars, their hands, backs, breasts, belly, thighs and God knows what else

Birthmark, 1997,
photo and ink by
Shirin Neshat (Iran)
Courtesy of Shirin Neshat

decorated with intricate designs in henna. The Artist-Formerly-Known-As-Prince has appeared in several of his recent concerts with his hands adorned in similar fashion. Madonna's hands were hennaed for the video of Frozen, her latest hit from the recently released album Ray of Light. Demi Moore has tried henna painting, and Mira Sorvino was widely reported when she appeared with henna decorated hands at a recent gala organised by the American Film Institute. Super model Naomi Campbell, who bared henna-decorated shoulders in a recent issue of Harper's Bazaar, is reported as having her feet decorated on a regular basis. Gwen Stefani, lead singer of the band No Doubt, is rarely seen in public without elaborate henna designs on her hands and belly, or a bindhi on her forehead. The British singer Sting and his wife, both Yoga lovers, have been known to have Zen 'Mehndi evenings' with an artist on hand to decorate their guests with henna.[2]

But the rage for henna is not confined to glossy photo-spreads in popular magazines. In London, one recent afternoon as I strolled down Leicester Square, I noticed a large crowd of young British women, all of them clad in fashionable black, queuing to have their hands, feet, and other body parts decorated with henna. Among the artists who executed these designs was a young Sudanese woman. She works for a young Cape Verdean entrepreneur who advertises her Sudanese national origin, and by extension her closeness to the tradition of henna, as 'getting the authentic thing'!

One could go on citing the increasing number of books published on henna art in the last two years, the catalogues of henna design, and Do-It-Yourself-Manuals, not to mention the endless media coverage, the henna parties, shops, saloons, and galleries specialising in henna decoration. And alas! The art of henna has even entered cyber space. At the time of writing, there are more than twenty web sites, lists and chat rooms dedicated to the art of henna. In short, henna has taken the Western world by storm! The question is: 'why?'

The answer to this question is very complex. In order to understand it, we will need to explore the art of henna in its traditional contexts, especially in Africa and Asia, where it has been for centuries a part of local tradition. We will also need to understand the origin and evolution of the Western fascination with non-western cultural products; a fascination which contrasts sharply with the West's traditional contempt for non-western people, and the mixture of desire and fear towards them.[3] This will help us to understand not only the current popularity of henna art in the West, but also the anger voiced by some vocal members of non-western immigrant communities in the West who regards the current fad as an act of appropriation.

This essay will explore these issues by referencing the work and life story of Setona, a Sudanese artist now based in Cairo whose henna art has gained international recognition in the last two years. Setona's work will then be compared to practices of various commercial entities in the West, where the appropriation of these ancient forms has considerably profited its entrepreneurs.

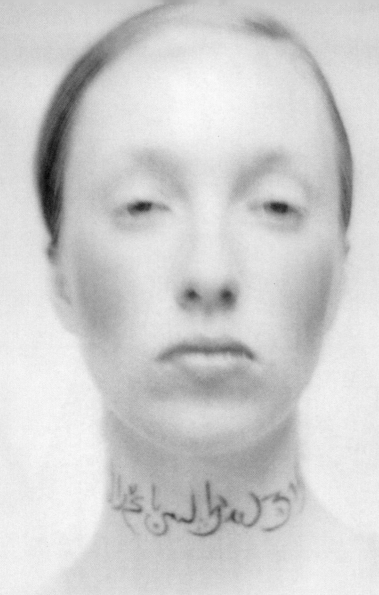

Make-up and hair by Mo Karadag for
House of Orange, Amsterdam, the Netherlands
© of the photographer: Anna Tiedink/NEL,
Amsterdam, the Netherlands

The hands of the bride
Photo Studio Gulf, Marrakech, May 1991
Courtesy of Mariëtte van Beek, Amsterdam,
the Netherlands

HENNA BODY PAINTING: TRADITION IN CONTEXT

One of the most ancient cosmetics known to human society, henna is a paste made of dried and pulverised leaves of the Lawsonia inerm, a small shrub found in Africa, Australia, and Asia. Though recipes vary from one society to another, the henna is most commonly mixed with ingredients such as water and eucalyptus oil.[7] Henna derives its name from the Persian, but is also used in many other languages to refer to the tradition of body art with which it is associated. The henna plant comes in a variety of fragrances and colours. Many scholars trace the plant's origin to Egypt, where the earliest evidence of its use has been found. Ancient Egyptians used henna to decorate their fingernails, and traces of henna have been found on the hands of Egyptian mummies and the decoration of burial costumes.

Henna decorations are normally accomplished by applying elaborate designs and patterns on the feet and hands. The result is intricate and aesthetically pleasing designs ranging in colour from red to dark brown, and lasting anywhere from seven days to a month. The exact shade depends on the length of time the paste is left to dry on the skin and on the extra ingredients which are added to it. Preference for henna colours ranges from reddish brown in India and Morocco to dark brown or black in Sudan, where certain ointments and incense are used to create this effect.[8] Unlike tattooing or scarification, the process is painless and leaves no permanent trace, a major factor in its appeal to Westerners.

It is important to note that henna painting is not popular among dark-skinned Africans, especially in sub-Saharan parts of Africa. The monochromic pigment and linear-patterned henna designs normally show up better in lighter skinned populations. Hence, scarification and cicatrisation tend to be typical of sub-Saharan Africa. However, henna is popular in some parts of East Africa, such as the coastal regions of Tanzania and Kenya, or West Africa in such places as Senegal, Mali and Nigeria. There, the decorations are generally confined to the lighter parts of the body, such as the palm of the hands or the soles of the feet. One exception to this is the less permanent polychromatic forms of body decoration adopted by dark-skinned Africans, whereby the skin is treated like a canvas for brightly coloured designs, as in the example of Nuba male body painting.

As an ancient artistic tradition, henna has evolved an elaborate material culture in terms of recipes, preparations, and the tools with which the henna is applied. Tools can vary from simple cones to recent innovations such as syringes and tubes which squeeze the paste onto the body. Preparation of the body involves removal of skin hair and the washing and annointment of all areas of the body destined for decoration. As in the other plastic arts, this creates a smooth, moisturized canvas for the application of the designs.

Thanks to its new popularity in the West, henna body painting has gone contemporary. One can now walk into a variety of popular retail stores and confidently scan the shelves for take-home henna kits with step-by-step instructions and a wide choice of stencil designs. Over-the-counter

At a wedding in Raf Raf, Tunisia, 1960

© Nja Mahdaoui, Tunis, Tunisia

Artist Nja Mahdaoui during a performance with Canadian actress and dancer Miryam Montillet, 1996
© Njah Mahdaoui, Tunis, Tunisia

tubes of henna paste are also available with a shelf-life of more than three weeks, in comparison to the traditionally prepared paste which looses its dyeing quality after three days.9 The trendy Body Shop offers The-earth-henna-body-painting-kit, complete with eucalyptus oil, stencil and powder and over 25 designs.

As a predominantly feminine art, the tradition of henna painting has been passed down orally from one generation of women to another, with daughters learning from their mothers, aunts, older relatives, and neighbours. Though a communally-oriented art with sets of traditional symbols and designs, henna is largely an improvisational art where originality and individuality are highly appreciated. It is also fashion-oriented, where newer designs easily replace the outdated ones.

In these cultures, henna art remains largely associated with the rites of initiation into womanhood.10 This is why the most elaborate designs are executed during the rites of passage associated with puberty, circumcision and the celebration of marriage. In some societies, such as Northern Sudan, the bride-groom may have his hands and feet decorated with less elaborate designs the night before his wedding (Laylat al hinna), but it remains a feminine art form.

In North Africa and Asia henna is known for its healing and medicinal qualities. It conditions the skin at the same time as it beautifies it. The list of henna's uses is very long. Its value as an antiseptic for bruises and wounds, its cooling qualities for the feet and hands in hot climate, and its healing properties for many skin and internal diseases, are well known. Henna is also used for dyeing leather and cloth and for decorating walls and animals.

Henna painting is an intricate part of the mythology of ancient Hinduism, Judaism and Islam, and the theories of its origin can be found in elaborate stories woven into the belief systems of their popular traditions.11 Henna is known for its magical and protective qualities. In Morocco, certain henna designs are believed to protect its wearer from the evil eye. In Morocco and Sudan, women sometimes throw a henna party for a new mother, or seek to placate a spirit in the context of rituals associated with Zar.

As art, henna has its own language of designs and symbols. Of course the meaning assigned to these symbols and designs can vary from one culture to another. The patterns and motifs which constitute these symbols are inspired not only by local belief but also by aspects of the indigenous flora and fauna. In short, the signs and symbols which constitute the language of henna art can only be deciphered in relation to the belief system of a specific culture, and through an intimate knowledge of the culture in question.12

Today, the most elaborate henna designs are practiced in Sudan, Morocco and India, where the tradition has been elevated to a serious art with its own class of full-time professional artists. Today, with henna gone global, several artists from these countries have begun to enjoy the patronage of the rich and famous in Europe and North America.

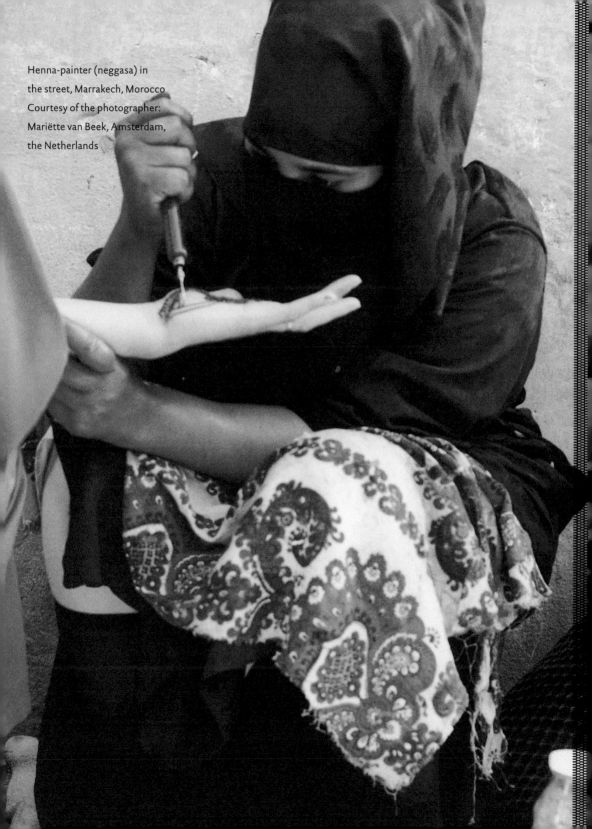

Henna-painter (neggasa) in
the street, Marrakech, Morocco
Courtesy of the photographer:
Mariëtte van Beek, Amsterdam,
the Netherlands

The-Artist-Formerly-Known-As-Prince
Photo: Steve Park
Courtesy of BMG, Hilversum,
the Netherlands

BODY ART: ORIGIN AND FUNCTION

Body decoration is among the least studied genres within African and non-western art scholarship. In a market-driven discipline, which early in its history catered largely to the interests of Western collectors, the study of body decoration was not profitable, i.e.'fundable'. The reason, body art is simply not collectable. In the case of African art studies, the field has remained largely a Western discipline, a product of Western sensibility and an expression of Western aesthetic responses to African visual culture. Hence, scholars of African art have primarily focused on collectable forms such as sculpture, egregiously neglecting body decoration despite the crucial role it plays in the life of many African societies.

With the recent shift in the art market and the new focus on entire genres of artistic practice, scholarship has changed accordingly.[4] The flourishing market of henna painting is a case in point. The striking number of recent books on henna art and other non-western forms of body art such as jewellery and costumes are testimony to their viability in the market place.

Not surprisingly, decorating or altering the body is a part of every human society. After all, the body 'is the medium through which we most directly project ourselves in social life; our use and presentation of it say precise things about the society in which we live, the degree of our integration within that society and the controls which society exerts.'[5] Like language and ritual practices, body decoration serves to set people apart from one another.

In Africa, where body art takes elaborate form, the body can be adorned in ways that range from permanent alterations such as tattooing, scarification and cicatrisation to more temporary forms, such as henna and other forms of body painting, hair styling, clothing, and jewellery.

Of course, the most obvious reason for decorating the body is beauty. It serves to enhance one's natural appearance and to give the impression of beauty, strength and good health. In many African and Asian societies, body decoration is an integral part of the rites of passage ushering the individual into a new way or status in life, such as birth, marriage or death. Among the Nuba in Sudan, use of color and design delineate age groups from birth to old age. Younger men are restricted to simpler hairstyles and red ochre, while adults between the ages of 17 and 27 years are allowed a full range of vibrant colors and designs and a variety of elaborate hairstyles. After this, men decorate themselves in black and ochre until old age when painting and decoration ceases altogether, since the body is no longer considered attractive.[6] Styles of coiffure can signal that a woman is single, married, pregnant, or in state of mourning. In several regions of West Africa, people consider the head not only the seat of wisdom, but of power as well.

In many parts of Africa, permanent body alterations such as scarification are often done to emphasise membership in certain ethnic, religious or social group. That is to say, body decoration serves as a public marker of ethnicity, identity and personal allegiance to a particular group.

Henna design by Setona, Cairo, Egypt
© of the photographer: Martin Riedel,
Berlin, Germany

Setona
© of the photographer:
Martin Riedel, Berlin, Germany

SETONA: THE NATIVE HENNA ARTIST IN A GLOBAL CONTEXT

Setona, a henna artist from Sudan, is probably the best-known and most internationally marketed henna artist. Setona's story exemplifies the destiny of an artist in a changing world characterised by massive human mobility, dislocation, and globalisation. Hers is also the story of resilience and success in the face of all odds. After all, being a woman and an artist in a place where such a profession lacks the respectability it deserves, this is a remarkable achievement. Setona, whose real name is Fatma Ali Adam Uthman, was born in the province of Kordofan in western Sudan. She moved with her family to Khartoum, the capital of Sudan, when she was a child. Given the fact that she hails from a family of well-known musicians, it is not surprising that her first profession is really that of a singer and musician.[13] Since 1989, Setona has been living in Cairo, Egypt, probably one of the many creative individuals forced to flee Sudan in the wake of that country's oppressive regime. She lives in the neighbourhood of Al Halamiya with her husband, Ahmed, formerly a teacher in the Sudan as well as a musician who accompanies her in public performances with the lute, the popular Sudanese string instrument. Setona's music combines folk and contemporary Sudanese music with the traditions of women's lore and wedding songs.

Setona has been credited, and with good reason, with the revival of henna body painting in Egypt. She may not be the only Sudanese henna artist in Cairo, but she is certainly the most celebrated thanks to her many artistic talents and entrepreneurial sophistication. What distinguishes Setona is her ability to market herself as a wedding consultant for 'Sudanese retro-style' ceremonies, where she starts by applying the henna designs on the bride and teaching the women Sudanese dances, and ends with singing traditional songs during the ceremony itself. Setona's expertise in the traditional body care of Sudanese women known as Dukhan (vapor-bath) and Bakhur (the burning of incense to perfume the body) are also in demand.[14] In other words, Setona draws on her knowledge of an entire set of traditions associated with body care and body painting in the context of Sudanese wedding rites.

Setona's considerable artistic and entrepreneurial success can be measured in many ways. Her skill in the art of henna painting has earned her the title of 'Queen of Henna' in Egypt, and the demand for her work is world-wide. Among her most famous clients is The-Artist-Formerly-Known-As-Prince, who reportedly, makes special trips to Cairo in order to be decorated by Setona. Five-star hotels in Cairo, such as the Meridian, Sheraton, and Hilton, book Setona well in advance for special wedding parties.[15]

Lately, Setona has taken to the stage, performing with the avant-garde Egyptian theatrical group El Tali'aa, the Vanguards. She even had a minor cameo role in one of the most successful Egyptian movies in recent years, 'An Upper Egyptian in The American University.'[16]

Setona's remarkable success in Egypt is not always viewed favorably by many of the exiled Sudanese intellectuals in Cairo. Some have criticised the Egyptian fascination with Setona as an act of appropriation that exoticises and stereotypes Sudanese culture.[17] They compare the Setona phenomenon with the Western appropriation of African cultural products. Interestingly, many seasoned Sudanese musicians and singers, such as Mohammed Wardi and Mohammed El Amin, whose styles have defined modern Sudanese music for the last thirty years, and who have been residing in a voluntary exile in Egypt for the last ten years, never enjoyed Setona's success. Setona's popularity has also been attributed to the shift in Egyptian identity as Egyptians move away from pan-Arabism towards increasing awareness of their African heritage.[18]

Setona's international success must also be attributed to her shrewd entrepreneurial skills. Nevertheless, she could never have achieved such popularity without the current rise of henna art and African music in the West. Interestingly, her brochures and CD write-ups market her as the 'Black Magic Woman'. Such labeling is very revealing of Western marketing strategies and their capitalisation of the 'exotic', the 'magical', and the 'primitive' so popular in the West. Thus, Setona's success becomes more comprehensible when read within the context of the henna mania sweeping the West today.

BODY ARTS AND THE WEST

Despite the sudden craze, henna is not entirely new in the West. For many years now, henna has been used in the West as a hair colour and as an ingredient in shampoos and hair conditioners. Due to the relative invisibility of non-western immigrant communities in the mainstream media, it is easy to forget that henna has never gone out of use by these communities in their adopted land. In weddings and other celebrations across Europe and North America, women from North Africa and India have continued to decorate their bodies with henna designs. For many years, whether in Liverpool, London, New York or Los Angeles, the ingredients for henna painting have been available in Middle Eastern, Indian and other so-called 'ethnic' specialty stores.

Henna art took the fashion world by storm beginning in early 1996. Carine Fabius, author of a book on henna art and the owner of a gallery dealing in henna painting, attributes the success of henna to the fact that it offers 'a safe, painless, and socially acceptable way of tattooing oneself at a time when the art of permanent tattooing (has reached) its peak.'[19] She also points out that henna emerged on the scene just at the time when India was enjoying a period of renewed interest in the West, sparked by the renaissance of Indian literature, film and fashion that marked India's fiftieth anniversary of independence. According to Fabius, it was a matter of 'the right product at the right time and the right place; and probably the Mehndi gods were ready!'

In order to fully understand the sudden popularity of henna body painting in Europe and North America, it is important to explore the evolution of Western attitude towards non-western body art forms. According to most scholars, Europeans first became aware of the different forms of body art practised by African, Asian, or Native Americans early during the so-called 'Age of Explorations', from the late fifteenth century onward.[20] But it is not impossible that the Europeans became aware of North African and western Asian body traditions at an even earlier date. Be this as it may, the body traditions of other cultures increasingly entered the Western consciousness thanks to the rise of anthropology, the invention of photography, the emergence of mass media, and the hosts of other factors put to the service of colonial interests. Yet, Arnold Rubin argues, this new consciousness did not lead immediately to appreciation of the diversity of human ways and cultures. In contrast, it led to reinforcement of the sense of superiority among Europeans and persistence of the stereotype of the naked savage as 'dark and ominous, with bones in his nose and pierced earlobes, and strange figures incised into his skin.'[21] The famous world fairs at the turn of the century and the natural history museums filled with collections of artifacts from conquered populations all served to reinforce these stereotypes.

These perceptions, though not yet rooted out, have begun to fade since the 1950s and 1960s, following the rise of independence movements among Third World nations and the demand for increased control over their own destinies. Since then, other factors have contributed to the positive attitude towards non-western body arts. As noted by Arnold Rubin, exchange programs with Third World countries, such as the Peace Corps and other volunteer projects, made it possible for many young Westerners to experience these cultures more intimately. The Hippie movement in the 1960s, and later on the Gay and women's liberation movements in the 1970s and 1980s have drastically changed Western attitudes towards the body through adoption of non-western body norms, from the piercing of body parts to tattoos and hairstyles.[22]

The increasing visibility of non-western immigrant communities, in addition to the struggle for minority and immigrant rights, have inaugurated a movement towards multiculturalism in Western societies. This in turn has led to a better understanding and appreciation of non-western cultural norms and customs, including, of course, body arts.

There are other kinds of movements which have expanded the appreciation of non-western body arts. These include the environmental and ecological movements and the increasing interest in alternative medicine, homeopathy, and Eastern spirituality. One can easily notice in the 1990s that such impulses add up to a longing for the sacred that seems to cut across much of Western culture. For centuries Westerners have turned to the East for spirituality to satisfy such longings. Spiritual impulses may indeed be a private matter. As brilliantly articulated by Jon Pareles, in the New York Times of June 21, 1998, spirituality in the West is 'a loose and open-ended term; it has been applied to Trappist monks and to people who meditate for a few moments between cut-throat negotiating sessions.' As the year 2000 approaches, Pareles argues that a looming sense of 'pre-millennial reckoning' reminds Westerners that 'something is missing from their worldly-oriented and materialistic life.' At the center of this spirituality is the idea that other cultures may have preserved something forgotten, or provide some unknown solution to problems at home. Hence, the appropriation of spiritual items from remote and unfamiliar places evokes a longing at the same that it provides a justification for multiculturalism.

HENNA MANIA: APPROPRIATION, OR AN INNOCENT ACT OF APPRECIATION?

Throughout much of this century, Western artists in all fields, from painting, sculpture, dance, music, fashion and design, have learned a great deal from the so-called 'primitive'. Today, such practices of appropriation, reinterpretation (or even misinterpretation!) have gained currency due to the common belief that the people dubbed 'primitive' by the West preserve ancient ways that may yet have something to offer or inspire creative innovations.

As I have argued elsewhere, the Western world has learned to modulate its language and to soften its objectifying discourse in relation to African and other non-western cultures.[23] However, racial determinism and the demand for exoticism and displays of authenticity remain central to Western criteria of representation and the validation of non-western cultural products. The history of representation of non-western cultures and arts in the West has traditionally served to legitimise the cultural, political and economic agenda of the establishment. There is a real danger in the way henna body art is represented in the West. It packages group identity in a manner that more often than not results in gross misrepresentations and in new kinds of stereotypes.

Power is the basis of cultural appropriation and interpretation. The dominant groups in society have the power to represent other groups through their control of the media, education and other institutions. Even under the best circumstances, such representations are all too often an over-simplification of a complex people and culture, in a way that hinders understanding between groups. Therefore, it should not come as a surprise that the celebration of henna art by Western celebrities has generated a sense of resentment among intellectuals and critics who belongs to immigrant groups for whom henna body painting is part of a tradition and cultural heritage.

Sherry Chopra, a Canadian of Indian descent, writes: 'The fact that aspects of a minority culture must be first legitimised by a white person to be accepted is an example of racism. The bindhi, which for years has been ridiculed as a 'paki dot', is now at the height of fashion, and worn by white girls and women, and some men. It is acceptable because it has been made so by white celebrities.'[24]

Chopra identifies the 'India trend', including the henna craze, as escapism, and an attempt by people who feel 'trapped in a society generally lacking meaning and community bonds, and governed by rules of consumption, to find meaning in their lives'. As she correctly argues, a void created by consumption cannot be filled through consumption of other cultures. When interest in India or Africa becomes passé, the commodified cultural products of their cultures will also be discarded, and people will move on to the next fad. Chopra cites the resentment among Hindu communities in Canada following the recent appearance of Madonna on an MTV awards presenta-tion, as the star performed one of her provocative acts while wearing henna, a see-through top, and the Hindu religious mark of purity on her forehead.

Chopra's criticism echoes an earlier essay by bell hooks entitled 'Madonna: Plantation Mistress or Soul Sister?' in which hooks criticises similar acts of appropriation.[25] Hooks characterises white

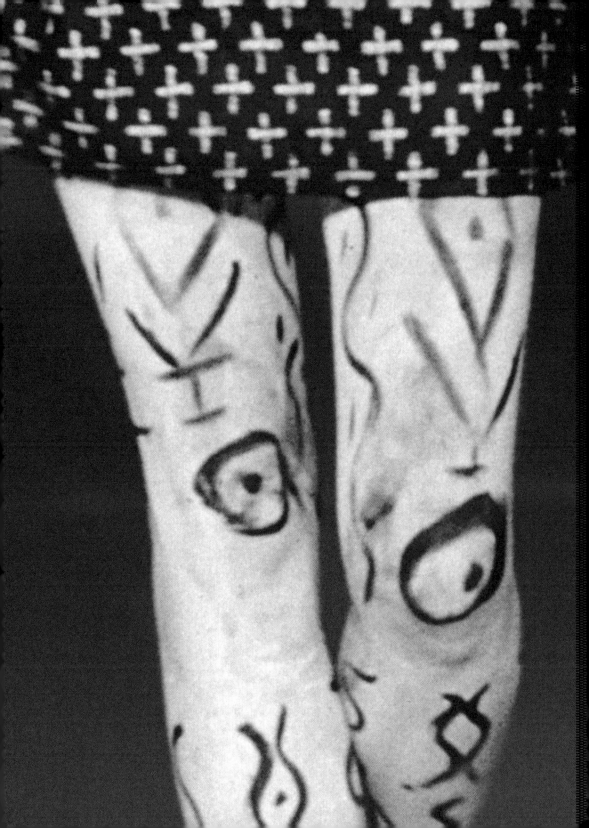

women stars like Madonna, who show their interest in, and appropriation of, black culture as yet 'another sign of their radical chic'. She argues that 'intimacy with 'nasty' blackness good white girls stay away from, is what Madonna and her likes seek'. It is this association which gives white and other non-black consumers that extra spice. As hooks states: 'After all it is a very recent historical phenomenon for any white girl to be able to get mileage out of flaunting her fascination and envy of blackness. The thing about envy is that it is always ready to destroy, erase, take-over, and consume the desired object. That is exactly what Madonna attempts to do when she appropriates and commodifies aspects of black culture.'[26]

The appropriation of body painting and other traditions can of course be used for entirely different purposes. It might be argued that many African and Asian artists engage in their own acts of appropriation when they use their own traditions in order to reach a global audience. But such appropriation can also be seen as an attempt to enter into a dialogue with one's own culture and history, motivated by the need to create new visual vocabulary of iconography, symbolism and technique.

Artists working within a conceptual post-modernist mode have engaged in acts of appropriation to emphasise, subvert or throw irony, on their own self-referentiality. Such are the modes of expression deployed by Shirin Neshat, an Iranian-born New York-based artist who explores the paradox in which the women of her native country live today. Neshat is intrigued by the relation of the female body to the politics of Islam and the way in which woman's body has been a type of battleground for various kinds of rhetoric and political ideology. Her 'Allegiance With Wakefulness' (1994) is part of a series of photographic works in which Neshat is specifically concerned with the participation of Iranian women in the military during the devastating Iran-Iraq war. In her 'Birth Mark' (1997), 'Identified' (1997), and 'Stories of Martyrdom' (1994), Neshat consciously alludes to the tradition of henna body painting as practised by women in Iranian society for various types of festivities and rituals. She uses the images of the gun, women's bodies, the veil and calligraphy to heighten the tension between the physical paradoxes of symbols and objects. Here the choice of texts on women bodies – women's poetry inscribed in calligraphy on their faces, hands and feet in a manner reminiscent of henna decorations – becomes critical in communicating the idea of multiple layers of information and reality.[27]

Similarly, one can also analyse the work of Farid Belkahia, a pioneer Moroccan modernist who has used henna and traditionally inspired designs in his work. To his credit, Belkahia undertook serious research into the potent modernity of some forms of the traditional arts of Morocco. Belkahia's endeavor was motivated by his keen interest in memory, which tends to play a central role in his identity and in his creative process as an artist. In a series of works entitled 'Hand' (1980), Belkahia uses henna dye on lamb skin in a way that evokes traditional techniques such as tattooing and henna body art in Morocco. The choice of such colours is motivated by his desire to be close to earthy colours. When treated with natural pigments such as henna, lamb skin takes on a range of colours from red to the dark browns.

CONCLUDING REMARKS

The renewed interest in henna body art in the West offers a unique opportunity to reflect on artistic practices in this age of massive mobility, dislocation, and globality. It causes one to rethink traditional conceptions of art and aesthetics, perceptions of the body, the culture of sex and desire, and above all, fashion as a statement and a public display of the self.

In the end, what makes the revival of henna body painting in the West most interesting is the contradictory and almost paradoxical context in which it is taking place. On one hand, there has certainly been a growing interest since the mid-eighties in African art in particular, and in non-western art in general.[28] On the other hand, this growing interest is taking place in a Western world (Europe and North America) that is becoming increasingly xenophobic and bent on closing its borders to African and Asian immigrants. The curb on immigration, the recent Draconian laws in the United States and Europe, and the neo-Nazi attacks on African and Turkish refugees in Germany are but a few examples of such xenophobia. The adoption of henna arts gives the appearance of celebrating diversity and multiculturalism. We can certainly give credit to the forces of globalisation and internationalism within the art world which have led to some accommodation of marginalised people's arts. Whether this will dismantle the Western power base and hegemony any time in the foreseeable future, however, is doubtful.

NOTES

1.

Aida Kanafani; *Aesthetics and Ritual in the United Arab Emirates*, Beirut American University, Beirut, 1983, p. 6

2.

The British daily Sunday Telegraph (August 2, 1998)

3.

Said, Edward W.; *Orientalism*, Pantheon Press, New York, 1978, Torgovnick, Mariana; *Gone Primitive*, University of Chicago Press, Chicago, 1990 and Fanon, Frantz; *Black Skin, White Mask*, Pluto Press, London/UK, 1986

4.

Rubin, Arnold (editor); *Marks of Civilization, Artistic Transformations of the Human Body*, Museum of Cultural History, University of California, Los Angelos, 1988 is a ground breaking work in the area of body arts.

5.

Ebin, Victoria; *The Body Decorated*, Thames and Hudson, New York, 1979, p. 5

6.

Faris, James; *Nuba Personal Art*, Duckworth, London/UK, 1972

7.

The most common ingredients are: powdered and sifted henna leaves, eucalyptus oil, black tea, and of course water for mixing with lemon. For more recipes see: Roome, Lorretta; *Mehndi, The Timeless Art of Henna Painting*, St. Martin's Griffin, New York, 1998 and Fabius, Carine; *Mehndi, the Art of Henna Body Painting*, Three Rivers Press, New York, 1998

8.

To achieve the preferred darker brown and black henna designs, Sudanese henna artists usually add a black hair dye to the henna paste. Health officials have campaigned against this practice since the dye is toxic to the skin. Today, some women add boiled tea to the mixture in order to achieve darker results.

9.

Fabius, Carine; *Mehndi the Art of Henna Body Painting*, op.cit., p. 31

10.

For more details see Saksena, Jogendra; *The Art of Rajasthan, Henna and Floor Decoration*, Sundeep Prakashan, Delhi, India, 1979 and Jereb, James; *Arts and Crafts of Morocco*, Chronicle Books, San Francisco, 1995

11.

Roome, Lorretta; *Mehndi: The Timeless Art of Henna Painting*, op. cit., p. 5

12.

Roome, Lorretta; *Mehndi: The Timeless Art of Henna Painting*, op. cit., chapter 2

13.

Setona's uncle, Omar Abdu, has been credited with founding the first kind of 'jazz bands' in Sudan; a Sudanese vocal music closer to what is known as R&B and Black pop music in the United States.

14.
The two types of body care function like a sauna. The woman sits over a hole in the ground covered with a blanket to get 'smoked'. It is important to note that these are traditions associated with the esoteric culture of sex and desire in Sudan.

15.
Setona has a German agent, Martin W. Riedel, who manages her international engagements and performances. Through Mr. Riedel's efforts, Setona has released two records on famous labels such as Blue Flame and BMG, and toured many of the major cities in Europe.

16.
Released the summer of 1998, the controversial comedy made box office history in Egypt, grossing more than a million dollars in its first few weeks.

17.
I would like to acknowledge the fruitful discussions I had with Adil Kibaida, a Cairo-based Sudanese artist during my recent visit to Cairo in the summer of 1998. Equally helpful were the insights and shrewd observations of Hassan Ali Ahmed and Safwat Ahmed, also of Cairo.

18.
The current debate among Egyptian intellectuals concerning the identity of Egyptian literature, culture and arts, and the renewed interest in Nubian culture and history, well illustrate this phenomenon. The interest in Sudanese culture and arts can be interpreted, therefore, as a kind of 'return to African roots.' Hence, the new popularity of Sudanese music, known for its faster tempo and hot rhythm, and the demand for henna and Sudanese-style weddings among fashionable Egyptian families. Gawhara, a Cairo-based Sudanese singer, has sold thousands of CDs of Sudanese folk songs and popular music, rearranged and written to suit popular Egyptian taste.

19.
Fabius, Carine; Mehndi, the Art of Henna Body Painting, op.cit. p. 32

20.
Rubin, Arnold (ed.); Marks of Civilization, op. cit. p. 14

21.
Ibid., p. 14

22.
Ibid., p. 14

23.
Hassan, Salah and Okwui Enwezor; New Visions, Six Contemporary African Artists, Zora Neale Hurston Museum of Art, Florida, 1994

24.
See Editorial, Ottawa Citizen, September 30, 1998

25.
hooks, bell; Black Looks, Race and Representation, MA: South End Press, Boston, 1992, p. 157

26.
Ibid, p.157

26.
Hassan, Salah; Genders and Nations, Herbert F. Johnson Museum of Art, Ithaca, 1998, p. 4

28.
Hence the proliferation of mega exhibitions, shows, festivals, and publications. To cite only a few examples: Africa 95, the British-based Festival of African Arts held during the Autumn of 1995; the Danish's Images of Africa festival, with its diverse multiple exhibitions and activities; and Africa, Art of a Continent at the Royal Academy in London, 1995 and at the Guggenheim Museum of Art, in New York, 1996.

Page 125

Design and body paint

by Katoucha, London, UK

Courtesy of Katoucha, Paris, France

Page 128

Hand, 1980, by Farid Belkahia (Morocco),

henna dye on lamb skin,

Mauritania, 1998

Courtesy of Farid Belkahia

Page 132

Detail old fabric (pagne) coloured with indigo, plangi and tritik technique from Saint-Louis, Senegal, private collection

Courtesy of Marie-Amy Mbow

Page 141

Wedding fabric, indigo coloured, from the Soninké people, Boké Diawé (Senegal), private collection

Courtesy of Marie-Amy Mbow

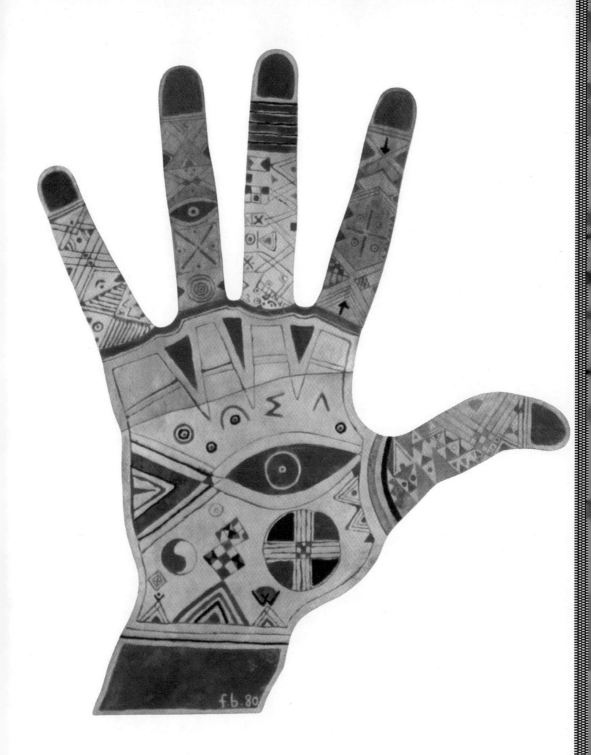

Madonna performs at the MTV Music Awards,
10 September 1998
Photo: Sam Mircovich
© Reuters

African

textile

design

MARIE-AMY MBOW

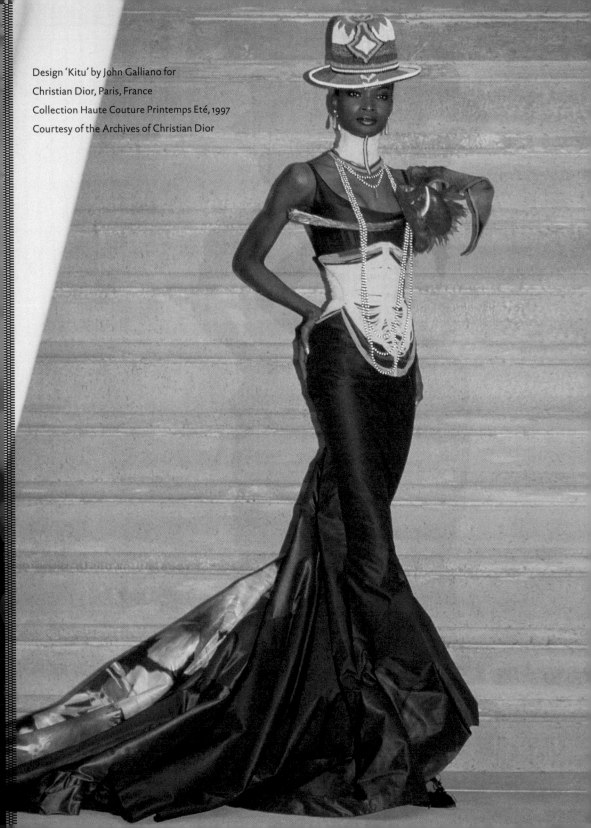

Design 'Kitu' by John Galliano for
Christian Dior, Paris, France
Collection Haute Couture Printemps Eté, 1997
Courtesy of the Archives of Christian Dior

January 1997 saw the launching of the leading fashion designers' spring and summer collections in Paris, fashion capital of the world. The British stylist John Galliano presented his first haute couture collection for Christian Dior, including Masai-inspired clothing designs and accessories in which beads, feathers and leather were combined. Dior first went exotic as long ago as 1969, with models parading the catwalk in turbans and muslim haïks. It was a time of immense variety in clothing styles (such as gypsy, Arab, Indian) through the worldwide hippy movement. Later, the Mediterranean designers Paco Rabanne and Azzedine Alaïa used long-limbed black models to show off their cross-cultural designs, which reflected the multiculturalism of the eighties and sowed the seeds of the future Benetton generation.

After serving for decades as an unacknowledged source of inspiration for designers and stylists around the world, Africa is now displaying its own styles and colours in Paris, now the mecca of such African fashion designers as Almen Djibirila, Gisèle Gomès, the late Chris Seydou (1949-1994, Mali) and Xuly Bët (Lamine Kouyaté, 1962, Mali). Africans are making their fashion accessible to the whole world by incorporating Western styles and standards, but at the same time offering entirely new colours, materials and blends. Each year more and more Africans find their vocation in fashion, trying their luck in Western capitals (which continue to be the main outlet for their products). They are confronted with real market conditions at fashion and textile shows and fairs, and are becoming aware of the unsuspected wealth of their cultural heritage and artistic potential.

Africa has a long and well-established tradition of varied, good-quality textile production, which is now the source of inspiration for African fashion designers.

TRADITION REVISITED, COSMOPOLITANISM AND IDENTITY IN AFRICAN FASHION DESIGN

Judging by the spread of tailors' signs in markets and on street corners in the various African capitals, the vitality of local textile manufacturing, and the richness and frequent modernisation of the clothes worn by fashionable young people in Dakar, Abidjan, Lomé or Libreville, there can be no doubt that fashion has many different facets. One is therefore justified in asking what it is that actually creates fashion in Africa.

Although Africans who belong to the small circle of 'leading fashion designers' would claim to be part of this movement, and indeed to have sired it, it is clear that true fashion – the fashion of the streets – is in fact created by local tailors or street-corner dressmakers and by fashionable young Africans themselves, for there are very few who can afford to wear African designer clothes.

However, Africa does have an admittedly fairly small number of 'fashion freaks' or 'dandies' whom have made it their vocation, or sometimes even their business, to be clothing consultants and arbiters of elegance. They have established a fraternity with its own special insiders' codes, and think of themselves as something of an aristocracy. They are to be found both in Africa and at the wellsprings of fashion – in Paris, Rome, Milan or London, wherever fashion is being created. They occasionally act as commercial advisers to leading fashion houses, preferably ones with

Canteen at the Tileen Market,
Médina, Dakar, Senegal
Courtesy of Marie-Amy Mbow

Italian, French or English names. They are usually men from former French or British colonies who have placed their love of elegant apparel at the service of their friends, acquaintances and clients. Their commercial acumen has, moreover, enabled them to establish showrooms and to sell leading makes of clothing on credit.

J-B. G., a 34-year-old Abidjan fashion consultant whose slogan is 'Les classiques ont une référence J-B. G.', always knows just what to wear at any time of the day or year, whatever the occasion. His top model is a famous radio and television host. The forerunners of this movement were undoubtedly the 'dandies' of Bacongo in Brazzaville.[1] In Bacongo, the members of SAPE (the 'Société des Ambianceurs et Personnes Elégantes', or 'Society of Makers of Atmosphere and Elegant People') offer a permanent spectacle in which they vie with one another for elegance with the help of designer clothes, 'tchatcho' colours, 'bali bali bachi' hairstyles, trousers with several creases, 501 jeans worn with knotted belts, and so forth. Their styles waver indefinably back and forth, embracing convention one moment and flouting it the next. Unlike the 'dandies' and 'snobs' who sought to shock the European bourgeois in the last century, SAPE members (known in French as sapeurs) follow fashion in order to assert themselves and acquire the external trappings of wealth and success in societies where appearance is all. While they are not fashion designers, they can certainly influence fashion, for with their reputations as elegant people they are admired and sometimes imitated, regardless of the quality of the clothes they are wearing. Thus, without always seeking to do so, sapeurs have brought about innovations in men's fashions in cosmopolitan Paris and Brussels, such as topees, certain kinds of hairstyle, baggy trousers with several creases, or khaki bermuda shorts with large pockets worn with plaited sandals or rope-soled shoes.

From a sociological viewpoint, behind the tricks of appearance in which the sapeurs indulge, one can detect a form of protest in their sartorial excesses and their distortion of the trappings of success – a way of scoffing at a social order, a government, a society in which they are unable to succeed through either work or study. Clearly, the main criticism levelled at these creators of fashion is that they consume Western products to the point of caricature, at the expense of local products, and that they are contributing to the decline of Africa's economy and culture. They are the result of a new cultural dynamic born of the encounter between Western and African culture, which has generated attitudes and behaviours that identify with the dominant model. According to Gandoulou[2], it is not mere cultural assimilation, but a more complex dynamic which leads sapeurs, depending on their abilities, personal resources and present expectations, to adopt appropriate behaviours and devise strategies to achieve their goals. In doing so, they innovate and create new standards by means of rituals and clubs – in other words, a sub-culture which they themselves did not foresee and which, in turn, determines and conditions their existence. The sapeur phenomenon shows that African cities are laboratories for innovation. New styles emerge and experimental social patterns adjust and readjust to them, with a certain amount of traditional input.

Designs with contemporary use of raffia by
Angybell, Senegal, shown at the Festival
International de la Mode Africaine, Niger, 1998

HISTORICAL BACKGROUND OF AFRICAN TEXTILES

We know about the history of African textiles from the study of private and public collections and especially from archaeology and from written sources. The antiquity of the art of weaving in Egypt, Sudan and West Africa has been confirmed by recent archaeological finds. In Ancient Egypt, the ruling elite and members of the court wore robes and tunics decorated with figurative and geometric patterns. One of the oldest pieces of fabric known to man is a pleated linen-fibre blouse or dress dating from the first Egyptian dynasty (approximately 3100-2890 BC). Similar tunics were among the items placed in the tomb of Tutankhamun (Pharaoh of the eighteenth dynasty, 1354-1346 BC). Cotton fabrics from Meroe in Sudan have been found in settings, which date back to the fifth century AD. At Igbo Ukwu in Nigeria, fragments of fabric made of bast fibre and raffia-like fibre have been found together with a large number of bronze sculptures and ornaments dating from the ninth to the eleventh century AD.

At Bandiagara in Mali, burial caves have yielded up fragments of clothing (tunics, trousers, hats, blankets and skirts) dating from the eleventh to the eighteenth century AD.3 These cotton garments, which were either left in their natural colour or dyed with indigo, were created by sewing strips of fabric together. They were decorated with simple embroidery (Kanaga patterns) or circular patterns obtained by tie-and-dye techniques. The fragments of woollen blanket found there resemble the North African Berber blankets (hambel, decorated with geometric symbols such as crosses, triangles and vertical bars) which were produced in southern Morocco and imported via the Sijilmasa trans-Saharan route from the ninth to the tenth century onwards.4

Writings by Arab and later Portuguese travellers allow us to establish the chronology of textiles in West Africa and on the Atlantic coast between the eleventh and the sixteenth century. From the eleventh to the fifteenth century, the wearing of garments became increasingly common among the Islamicised elite. In the eleventh century, the King of Ghâna (to the south of the present-day town of Walata, in Mauritania) and his courtiers wore cotton garments, whereas the majority of his people were half-naked or dressed in skins. According to Al-Bakri5, cotton was woven in the Senegal valley, and the so-called 'pagnes', cotton fabrics which can be used as skirts, were used as currency in the region. Textiles were brought in from southern Morocco via trans-Saharan trading routes and bartered for slaves and various other goods. In 1352, while visiting the court of Mansa Moussa, King of Mali (who made the pilgrimage to Mecca), the Moroccan traveller Ibn Batutta noted the richness of the costumes worn there, particularly at Friday prayers and during the feast to mark the end of Ramadan.

Trans-Saharan trade was in the hands of caravan traders, Berbers from the western Sahara known as Zenaga, and marabouts from the Kingdom of Fez or Morrocos6. The Wangara, who spoke Malinké and Soninké, carried on trade between Senegal and the interior of West Africa. These traders, who were Islamic Manden, also settled in the areas now occupied by Sierra Leone and Liberia and helped not only Islam but also the techniques of weaving and dyeing to spread

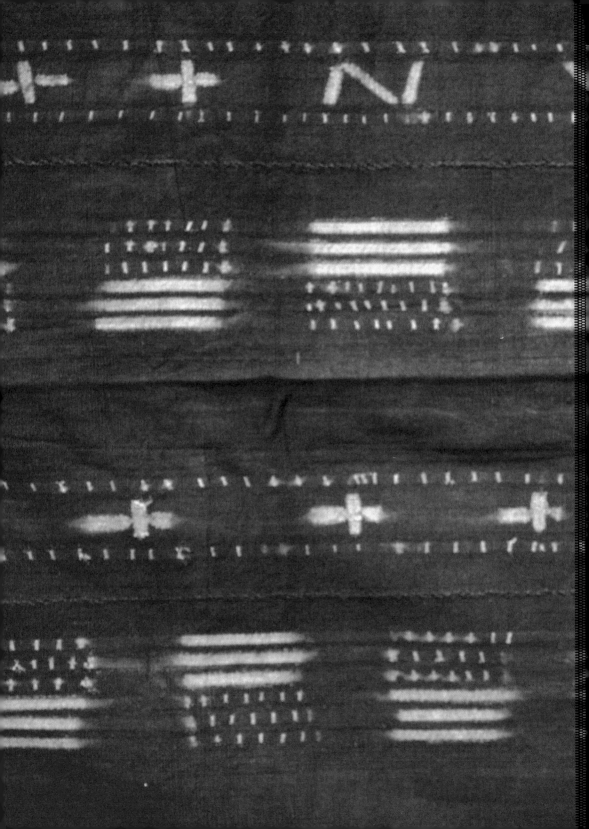

eastwards along the coast, from the Atlantic to Lake Chad. From the fifteenth century onwards the Portuguese embarked on their first seafaring expeditions along the African coasts, arriving on the coast of Senegal in 1444 and progressing further south each year. They maintained trading links with the places which they visited, especially sub-equatorial Atlantic regions such the Kingdom of Kongo (situated between present-day Congo-Brazzaville and Angola), where the use of textiles and the technique of manufacturing them from plant fibres were already known.

Between the fifteenth and the sixteenth century textiles became increasingly important as a medium of exchange, from Senegal to the bend of the Niger, from Agadez to the Kanem region, on the River Logone in Chad, from the Darfur to the Nile, and on the coasts of the Gulf of Guinea.

West Africa exported cotton fabrics from Gao and Djenné in Mali, and from Bornou to the south-east of Lake Chad. The Portuguese introduced cotton-growing to the Cape Verde islands and set up weaving-shops which were manned by slave workers from the mainland. Inspired by models from Moorish Spain and Africa, the textiles were sold along the African coast, in the Iberian Peninsula and elsewhere in Europe.[7]

The clothes worn around the mid-fifteenth century by people living along the River Senegal and the River Gambia were described by the seafarers Ca da Mosto, Duarte Pacheco Pereira and Valentim Fernandes.[8] The men wore thigh-length tunics with wide, elbow-length sleeves, and very loose, baggy trousers of various lengths, some reaching the ankle, others stopping at the knee; they also wore hats with ear-flaps. The women wore knee-length wrap-around skirts, but sometimes also long skirts which went all the way down to the ankle. People could dress very differently according to their rank, occupation or circumstances. There were also regional differences. Among the Wolof of Senegal, only the rulers and the wealthy were dressed in this way; everyone else wore goat-skin breeches. In the Gambia region, on the other hand, cotton garments were much more common.

In the seventeenth century the Portuguese textile industry declined, and woven products from the interior, particularly the Hausa region of northern Nigeria, now spread through major sub-Saharan towns as far as the equatorial forests to the south.

In the eighteenth century, for a time, locally produced cotton supplanted Afro-Portuguese products and other fabrics imported from Europe, India or Turkey. Then, in the late eighteenth and in the nineteenth century, European industrial fabrics such as 'guinée' (produced in the Indian town of Pondicherry by French manufacturers attempting to imitate African fabrics) and German, British and Dutch wax and java fabrics took over from local products, ushering in a colonial system of economic domination.

Old fabric (pagne), indigo, plangi and tritik technique,
possibly originally from Nigeria or Sierra Leone, private collection
Courtesy of Marie-Amy Mbow

Cultural group from Thiès (Senegal) wearing indigo
coloured pagnes made with the plangi and tritik technique
at the National Festival for the Arts and Culture in Thiès
Courtesy of Marie-Amy Mbow

FIBRE, TECHNIQUE, STYLE AND DYE

Most textiles in sub-Saharan Africa are made from plant fibres (bark, bast fibre, raffia, jute, linen and cotton); animal fibres such as wool and silk are seldom used. Synthetic yarns (lurex, rayon and polyester) are used increasingly often for their shiny effect.

Chemical dyes, with which an almost infinite range of colours can be obtained, have long since replaced indigo, kola and various extracts of leaves, roots, bark or minerals (mud rich in iron oxide) for use in dyeing yarns and fabrics. A yarn-dyeing technique known as ikat is practised in West Africa by the Dioula of Burkina Faso and Ivory Coast (particularly in Kong) and by the Yoruba of Nigeria. If the warp threads are dyed, this produces sharply defined patterns widthways and fraying or blurring lengthways.

There are several fabric-dyeing techniques – known as plangi, tritik and batik – which yield a wide variety of decorative patterns, in contrast to the rectilinear effects produced by weaving.

Plangi is a 'tie-and-dye' technique whereby one or more threads are used to tie off parts of the fabric very tightly. This prevents the dye from penetrating all the way through. Small pebbles, shells, or millet, cotton or indigo seeds may also be inserted. After the fabric has been dyed and dried, the tied-off parts are untied and patterns of circles, dots, discs, rings or diamonds appear. The same technique is practised with beaten bark (bamun, from Cameroon) and raffia fabric (dida from Ivory Coast, and kuba from Congo). The fabric may also be crumpled and squeezed in various directions, or alternatively folded into ordinary or twisted pleats, then tied off to create a multi-coloured or marbled effect. The possibilities afforded by this tie-and-dye technique are almost endless, and various methods may even be combined: such as crumpling and tying 'en galette', pleating and wringing, tying 'en boule' or 'en pointe', braiding and tying.

Tritik is a 'stitch-and-dye' technique in which three-dimensional areas are isolated by pleating, gathering or rolling so that the dye cannot penetrate. The stitching is done either by hand or by machine. Parts of the fabric may also be isolated by means of embroidery.

Batik involves applying millet or manioc paste, starch or (more recently) wax to the fabric by hand or by using various instruments (such as stencils, stamps, brushes, combs and spatulas) in order to create the pattern. After dyeing and washing, the pattern emerges. Bogolan, a technique practised by the Bamana women of Bélédougou, in Mali, is midway between batik and painting. Mud-based dyes are used to paint outlines, as opposed to the actual patterns, which remain colourless.

After dyeing, the fabrics are stiffened slightly with the help of starch or gum arabic. Once dry, they are folded lengthways and sent to be pressed by means of a technique known in Wolof as tapp. The fabric is laid on a convex block of wood which is completely flat on top, and is then beaten repeatedly with a cylindrical bat which is made of solid wood and has a handle at one end. A wax rod is rolled over the unstarched fabric beforehand to give it gloss, shine and finish.

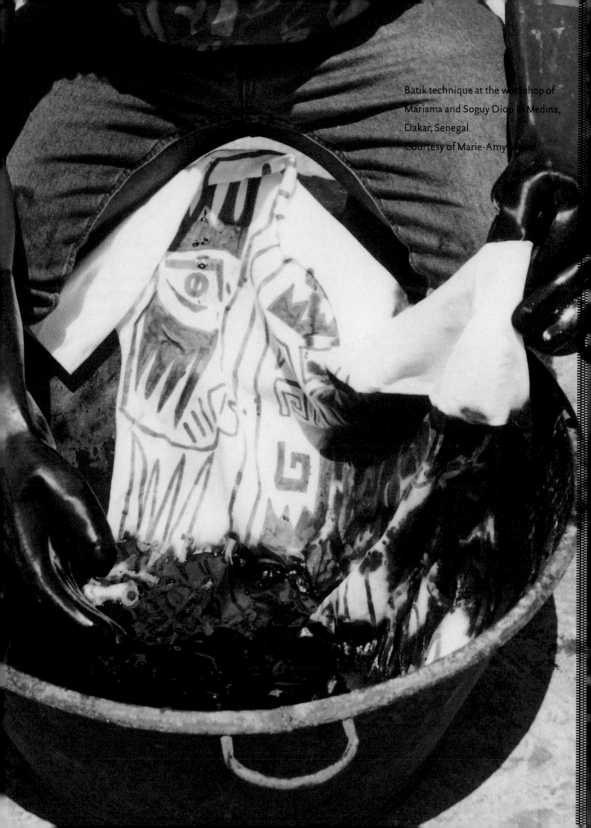

Batik technique at the workshop of
Mariama and Soguy Diop in Medina,
Dakar, Senegal
Courtesy of Marie-Amy Mbow

Display at a haberdasher's,
Dakar, Senegal
Courtesy of Marie-Amy Mbow

DRAWING AND PAINTING

Drawing and painting on fabric are not unknown in sub-Saharan Africa, but are seldom practised. Tunics covered with calligraphed texts (Arabic figures and letters, or geometric figures such as stars and squares), either drawn in ink or contained in sewn-up amulets, including verses from the Koran, are found in the Islamicised areas of the Sahel and western Sudan. These protective garments were reserved for leading dignitaries, warriors or hunters and all those who were confronted with force, danger and death in the course of their activities.[9]

The northern custom of wearing calligraphed garments was taken by the Ashanti of Ghana and incorporated, slightly modified, into their clothing tradition based on Adinkra fabrics. The art of bark-painting was chiefly practised in Central Africa, by the Mangbetu and the Bambuti of Congo, who used black, natural-coloured or ochre pigments to produce abstract patterns.

EMBROIDERY

Embroidery is a technique, which has become highly developed in Islamicised areas, especially the Hausa communities of Niger and Nigeria and at Djenné in Mali, as well as in Senegal and in Guinea. The embroiderers are usually readers of Arabic who have learnt their craft from their Koran teachers. The richly machine-embroidered boubous worn by men and women in all the West African capitals stem from this tradition.

There is also a kind of embroidery which Senegalese women use to decorate their pagnes. This kind of embroidery, which draws its inspiration from different sources, consists of traditional geometric patterns (such as diamonds, squares, herringbone) which are borrowed from woven fabrics. Certain figurative patterns are used to adorn sheets, hangings and pagnes like social scenes, floral compositions, mythical or famous figures (Mami Wata, Coura Thiaw), moral or political slogans and religious motifs (the horse of the Islamic prophet Al-Buraq). Such designs were often commissioned by the leading marabout families of Tivaouane and Touba, and the fashion spread among their disciples. The people of the Congo basin also have a well-established tradition of embroidery on raffia. The Kuba women, for example, give their embroidery a velvety appearance by inserting a strand of raffia at the intersection of a weft and a warp thread of an already woven fabric. The strand of raffia is pulled through on the right side of the material and cut off short at both ends. This juxtaposition of cut fibres creates a velvety effect. The appliqué technique was mainly practised in the ancient Fon kingdom of Abomey (where hangings decorated with appliqué patterns were used by the last kings as emblems) and in the Fanti states on the coast of Ghana. The Fanti states have traditional companies of warriors known as Asafo. Each company has a flag decorated with emblems that depict their mottos. The flags are displayed at the annual tournaments in which all the companies take part. This relatively recent tradition appears to have been copied from the British use of military banners.

Embroidered pagne, 1970s,
cotton from Mékhé (Thiès),
Senegal, private collection
Courtesy of Marie-Amy Mbow

Woven handbag, design by
Aïssa Dione, Dakar, Senegal
Courtesy of Marie-Amy Mbow

Show-window of a tailor and embroiderer of boubous, Médina, Dakar, Senegal
Courtesy of Marie-Amy Mbow

Weaving-mill of Aïssa Dione, in the
industrial area of Sodida, Dakar, Senegal
Courtesy of Marie-Amy Mbow

WEAVING

Several different types of loom are used for weaving, such as the horizontal fixed-heddle loom, mainly used in East and Southern Africa and Madagascar, the vertical fixed-heddle loom, used to weave raffia in Central Africa, and the treadle loom with suspended heddles and reed, the most widespread type in Africa (particularly West Africa), which can be used to produce extremely complex types of weaving (brocade, lancé, tapestry).

Although weaving is sometimes done by women (in North Africa, Madagascar and Nigeria), in Africa it is largely a male activity and is done mainly by certain socio-professional groups, particularly in West Africa. The best-known woven fabrics are the silk kente worn by Ashanti royalty and nobility in Ghana and Ivory Coast, the mandjak pagnes of Guinea-Bissau and southern Senegal, the ceremonial aso oke fabrics worn by the Yoruba in Nigeria, and the woollen kaasa blankets worn by the Peul in Mali.

These techniques – of which the above is not an exhaustive list – have been used to create a variety of patterns and combinations of patterns, mainly repetitive geometric compositions which lend harmony to the textiles and leave the weaver, embroiderer or dyer free to express himself artistically.

There is an evident similarity between the various African textiles, a similarity which is apparent at a regional level and is no doubt related to the history of the dissemination of textiles across the African continent. However, this similarity has certainly not precluded a proliferation of forms and styles which are constantly being renewed by the input of modern designs, processes and materials, simultaneously encouraging the emergence of new varieties of traditional African textiles.

TEXTILE DESIGN: TRADITION VERSUS MODERNITY

Tradition and African identity are the very sources which African fashion and textile designers exhibiting at the first K'palezo fashion show in Abidjan, Ivory Coast, in 1997 claimed to have drawn on. They emphasised the need to return to original traditional patterns, not in order to copy them slavishly, but to draw inspiration from them and to create original designs with the help of modern technology. The importance attached to traditional patterns, particularly in the field of textile design, was justified by the fact that they reflected African sensibilities and ancestral cultural values, which, in today's rapidly evolving world, needed to be acknowledged and highlighted. Admittedly, there is still considerable controversy as to the nature, content and present-day import of these values, but one thing is quite clear – namely, the awareness among most African designers that they are imparting an African sensibility to their designs, that they are inventing an identity of their own which is far removed from the artifices of conventional disguise, in short, that they are creating an authenticity based on work, meticulousness, creativity and merit.

Some examples of African design deserve special mention. For instance, there is the Ethiopian

Fabric and designs by Genet Kebede,
Addis Ababa, Ethiopia
Courtesy of Genet Kebede

Fabric and design by Genet Kebede,
Addis Ababa, Ethiopia
Courtesy of Genet Kebede

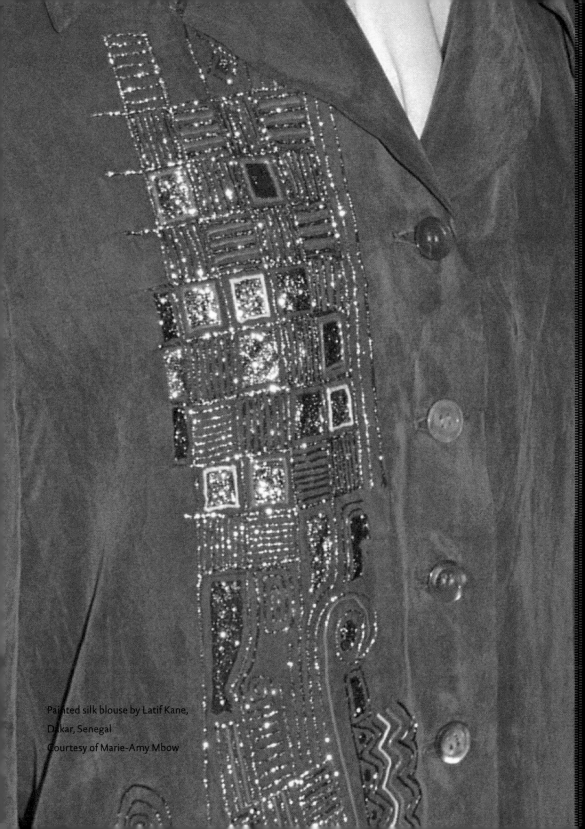

Painted silk blouse by Latif Kane,
Dakar, Senegal
Courtesy of Marie-Amy Mbow

stylist Genet Kebede, who in her Paradise Fashion atelier in Addis Ababa uses traditional cotton and silk tibeb fabrics, hand-woven by Shamane weavers and decorated with cross, star and line motifs, for her dresses and two-piece suits. Her evening dresses and velvet suits are embroidered in gold thread with geometric patterns borrowed from the kabba, ceremonial costumes worn by nobility and Orthodox clergy of the Ethiopean church; her velvet wedding dresses have patterns of flowers, leaves and symbols embroidered on them in gold thread. Genet Kebede works almost entirely with hand-made fabrics, and her unique, exclusive designs are drawn from Ethiopian cultural sources. Since 1993 she has taken part in various shows and exhibitions in Ethiopia, France (Salon du prêt-à-porter féminin, African Mosaïque), Germany (Igedo International Fashion Fair in Düsseldorf) and Ivory Coast (K'palezo).

In Senegal stylists also use traditional mandjak fabrics, hand-woven in cotton and silk threads, to make clothes. The most remarkable of these stylists are undoubtedly Collé Ardo Sow and Claire Kane, who are considered pioneers in this field. Both have ateliers in Dakar's Rue Mohammed V and factories which turn out original woven fabrics.

Originally from France, Claire Kane set up her own weaving factory in 1989. Since then she has focused on textile design, and her screen-printed patterns have earned her a solid reputation. Her flowing fabrics may be decorated with anything from CFA francs to visa stamps, tyre marks or 'at' signs (@); her garments, which are usually black or natural-coloured, are either ultra-brief or ankle-length. She was awarded the design show prize for creativity at the Dak'Art 98 Biennial exhibition.

Collé Ardo Sow, who comes from Diourbel, studied dressmaking in Senegal and then worked for leading French ateliers before settling in Senegal once again. She soon specialised in woven fabrics, making them supple and flowing enough to be used for dresses and suits. She has exhibited at numerous shows around the world, and for many years was one of the few designers from her country to attend them. Her designs are now synonymous with quality and creativity. In recent years her focus has shifted to textile design, and the unique, exclusive fabrics which she now markets have sustained her reputation. She is also innovating in machine embroidery and in nocci (openwork).

Also from Senegal, Aïssa Dione has concentrated on both furniture and textile design. She now markets a range of domestic linen, furnishings and various accessories (such as travelling bags, handbags, shawls and waistcoats). Her fabrics are woven on looms which can produce strips of fabric from 40 to 140 centimetres in width (whereas traditional strips are only 20 centimetres across). Her company is based in Dakar's Sodida business park and has a staff of about 100. She works for leading French design houses, particularly Hermès. An excellent user of colour, she has given a new boost to traditional weaving through colours, combinations of materials (raffia, cotton and silk) and tricks of texture (close or loose weave) rather than patterns. She has brilliantly demonstrated that Africa is capable of turning out high-quality textiles while making maximum

use of local materials and know-how. She has won several prizes at the Ouagadougou international handicrafts fair (SIAO) and regularly exhibits at international shows. Her products are now available in various African and European capitals.

Assita Tamboura, from Burkina Faso, makes a point of using products from her own country, such as faso dan fani (a traditional cotton fabric now woven at a factory in Ouagadougou from locally grown cotton), as the basis for her designs. Her blends of natural-coloured, dyed and geometrically patterned fabrics and highly becoming designs show local textiles to their full advantage.

Other stylists and designers have opted for a range that includes both locally manufactured fabrics and ones imported from Asia, America or Europe. Among them is Dasha Nikoué, from Benin, who settled in Dakar some twenty years ago. In 1997 she opened a huge atelier-boutique in the city centre. Using cotton printed in Senegal and Ivory Coast, she produces Western-style ready-to-wear designs from African fabrics. Her most original designs include dresses whose painted patterns are borrowed from the traditional patterns found on appliqué hangings in Abomey, Benin, batik dresses embroidered with gold thread, screen-printed linen outfits, or strapless raffia dresses. Dasha Nikoué is aiming at both international and local customers who, in times of economic difficulty, would prefer to spend less money on their clothes. In addition to her work as a stylist, she also designs for textile manufacturers and has launched a range of accessories (like shoes and bags).

Pathé O, a stylist and designer from Burkina Faso who is now based in Ivory Coast, uses various ranges of locally produced and imported fabrics, both hand-made and industrially manufactured. His latest collection, 'Sahel', which was presented at the gala of the 39th Organisation of African Unity summit in Ouagadougou in July 1998, was a blend of artistic wealth and simplicity; notable features included pastel tints, graphic blends of colour, and subtle accessories. His message was 'an appeal not to despair of the Sahel which, despite its climatic problems and economic difficulties, is a source of both human and cultural wealth.'

Laay Diarra is a fascinating character. He is considered almost a veteran in the Senegalese and African fashion world, for although still fairly young (43) he has worked in the garment-making business for very many years. He produces clothes for both men and women, and provides the perfect link between internationally reputed African designers and local tailors. He readily admits that he is a self-taught man from a traditional background and that he learned everything he knows the hard way, as a tailor's apprentice. With his vast technical experience, he has always been ready to break new ground in the field of design. He was the first to organise fashion shows as a means of promoting himself. He has attended numerous shows and exhibitions in other countries (such as France, Germany, Togo, Cameroon, the Gulf states and Pakistan). Laay Diarra is a level-headed, thoughtful man who shuns worldliness. His designs are simple and authentic, free of frills and superfluous artifice – clearly a reflection of his own genuine, principled nature. He regularly sets off into the field in pursuit of greater depth, balance and soundness. His men's clothing is a blend of conventionality, elegance and sobriety, with an ever-subtle African touch that brings out its virtuosity.

Urban Africans have a cosmopolitan identity which leads them to wear Western or traditional African clothes according to circumstances. This is particularly true of Senegal where, on Fridays, both Muslim and Christian men and women cast off their suits and dresses in favour of traditional boubous.

Senegal's leading lady in this area is without doubt Diouma Dieng, who designs richly embroidered (sometimes beaded) cotton and silk boubous, kaftans and outfits at her showroom-atelier. She draws inspiration from her many trips around the world, particularly to Asia, where she works with Pakistani embroiderers. Some of her designs are directly influenced by Moroccan caftans or Pakistani shawal-baz, which she reinterprets to suit her customers' tastes. Some of her boubous are painted by the La Médina-based artist Latif Kane, who also works for the stylist and designer Bineta Salsao, a specialist in woven fabrics. Latif Kane uses a special indelible paint to decorate cotton, silk, linen and leather. Young graduates from Dakar's College of Fine Arts, such as Mariama and Soguy Diop, from Dakar, are reinventing the art of batik in their atelier near the Sandaga market, turning out original artistic compositions which are a blend of African geometric symbols and figurative patterns and appear on such varied items as T-shirts, dresses, bathing costumes and tablecloths.

CONCLUSION

Textile design has not escaped the powerful innovative trend which can currently be seen all over Africa. While Africa's musicians and singers, in particular, are increasingly well-known in the main cities of Africa, Europe and America, its fashion designers are now projecting a whole new view of Africa, one very different from its front-page media image.

Despite the lack of creativity in textile design, despite the mimicing of patterns inherited from the colonial period and a still failing production apparatus, African fashion and textile designers are slowly but nonetheless surely establishing a place for themselves in the world of international fashion in a blend of craftmanship and art, flamboyance and simplicity, exuberance and sobriety, tradition and modernity.

NOTES

1.

Gandoulou J.; *Dandies à Bacongo, le culte de l'élégance dans la société congolaise*, Editions l'Harmattan, Paris, 1989

2.

Gandoulou; op.cit. 1.

3.

Bolland R.; *Tellem Textiles, Archaeological Finds from Burial Caves in Mali's Bandiagara Cliff*, Royal Tropical Institute, Amsterdam, 1991

4.

Gilfoy Stoltz, Peggy; *Patterns of life, West African strip-weaving traditions*, Smithsonian Institution, Washington DC, 1986.

5.

Al-Bakri; *Géographe andalou*, in: Cuocq, J.; Recueil des sources arabes concernant l'Afrique occidentale du VIIIe au XVIe siècle, CNRS, Paris, 1975.

6.

Fernandes V.; *Description de la côte occidentale d'Afrique de Ceuta au Sénégal, (1506-1508)*, Larose, Paris, 1938. French translation by P. de Cenival and T. Monod. And Fernandes V.; *Description de la côte occidentale d'Afrique (Sénégal, Cap de Monte, Archipels) (1506-1507)*, Centro de Estudos de Guiné Português, Bissau, 1951. French translation by T. Monod, A. Texeira da Mota and R. Mauny

7.

Boulègue J.; *Le grand Jolof (XIII-XVIe siècles)*, Editions Façades, 1987, quoting A. Carreira and A. Texeira da Mota: 'Milho zaburro and milho maçaroca in Guinea and in the islands of Cabo verde', Oxford Africa, Vol. XXXVI, No. 1, 1966

8.

Boulègue; op.cit.

9.

Coquet M.; *Textiles africains*, Editions Adam Biro, Paris, 1995

Page 161

Woman dress made of ikat fabric from Burkina Faso, design by Laay Diarra, Dakar, Senegal

Courtesy of Marie-Amy Mbow

Page 162

Woman dress of imitation bogolan from Lagos, design by Laay Diarra, Dakar, Senegal

Courtesy of Marie-Amy Mbow

Page 165

Musician Baaba Maal wearing a boubou at a concert in Cascas, Senegal, 1997 Baaba Maals' designer is Laay Diarra

Courtesy of PAOPIM/KIT, Cascas, Senegal/Amsterdam, the Netherlands

Page 167

Senegalese designer Pathé O and two models wearing his designs, Abidjan, Ivory Coast, 1998

Courtesy of Amina, Paris, France

Models!

RENÉE MENDY

Page 168, 174
Naomi Campbell
Courtesy of Elite, Amsterdam,
the Netherlands

Page 171
Iman
Photo: Sephytal S.A., Le Chesnay, France
Courtesy of Amina, Paris, France

Page 173
Yame
Courtesy of Name Models, Amsterdam,
the Netherlands

Page 175
Patricia Fotso, wearing jewellery by
Mickaël Kra from the collection
Reine Pokou on the cover of Amina
Courtesy of Amina, Paris, France

Iman, Mounia, Naomi Sims, Katoucha, Kimi Khan, Anna Getaneh, Naomi Campbell and Alek Wek are the black models of yesteryear and today. They represent the beauty of black women, each in her own way, each in relation to her own time. Why is it that whites are so keen on black women? The delicate, refined face of one, the dignified, graceful gait of another or the ethnic, raw characteristics of yet another. Whatever the reason may be, one thing is certain: whites have been smitten by jungle fever. These are good times for black women! A state of affairs which is set to continue.

Honour to whom honour is due. It is the year 1966 and we are in the United States. Paco Rabanne has just committed two disgraceful acts, both unheard of in the world of fashion. Before a hand-picked audience and the world press, the Spanish couturier has had his models parading to music. Surprise. Astonishment amongst the audience. But the most 'obnoxious' thing is the choice of models. Several of them are black. According to Paco Rabanne, the journalists from American Vogue rushed backstage at the end of the show to call him all the names under the sun. To spit in his face. He had only one reply: 'Black women are the most beautiful in the world'. A few collections later, Yves Saint-Laurent adopted Paco Rabanne's idea. He chose other models who were black, and beautiful, to take part in his shows. Without knowing it, Paco Rabanne had started a trend which was set to continue. The slogan 'black is beautiful' is now on everyone's lips.

Nowadays catwalks throughout the world are paraded by black models. They are enjoying great success. These are the models that are seen in fashion shows and in the most switched-on Western magazines. ID, the British magazine, and also Vogue and more recently Elle have put black girls on their covers. They are definitely in fashion, otherwise such magazines would not risk putting them on their covers and alienating their readers. Elle magazine is a perfect illustration of this new phenomenon. The women's magazine has highlighted the feline, raw beauty of Alek Wek throughout the whole of 1998. The young Sudanese model has been chosen for many leading fashion articles. To the great surprise of the blacks themselves – models or not – who have other criteria of beauty. The black models who are nowadays all the rage in the West are the very opposite of the women considered to be paragons of feminine beauty by Africans or Antilleans.

Pretty girls in Africa see all this from afar. From very far in fact. In their own African world they secretly dream of looking like Naomi Campbell. She is their reference point. They have but one obsession: to conquer Europe and become rich. Very few will succeed. Small modelling agencies are being set up, particularly in Abidjan and Dakar, the capitals of African fashion. But the clients are cruelly let down by the lack of contracts and sometimes by the lack of professionalism of the part of the 'agencies'. The market is so limited that only the most professional and persevering find work in a few shows. At the international events for African fashion creators, K'palezo, held in Abidjan, during the yearly fashion week in Dakar or during the FIMA International festival of African fashion in Agadez (1998). But the opportunities to mount the catwalk are only all too rare in Africa. The girls often lose heart, giving up even before they have begun.

One or two, however, do indeed stand out from the rest. Kimi Khan and Katoucha left the Ivory Coast and Senegal respectively to shine brightly in the West. At a very early stage they realised that if they wanted to conquer the world and fashion, they would have to captivate Paris. Kimi Khan had a splendid career in the early eighties. She was on the cover of many magazines, such as Amina, Ebony and Lui. She was the inspiration of famous European and American photographers. Above all, the beautiful Kimi became a star thanks to the Lee Cooper advertisements with Jean-Paul Gould (1985). In 1987 she represented the Pepsi image, as a statue of liberty. Inspired by the film Mad Max, the advertising poster was a success. And this was to be no exception for feline Kimi, as work came flooding in from all sides.

As for Katoucha, everyone will remember her as Yves Saint-Laurent's inspiration. He designed his most beautiful creations with this woman in mind, this Senegalese model of Guinean origin. The rolling gait of the girl affectionately known as Katouch' left the great couturier speechless. She too is a fine example of success in Paris. In the mid-nineties, Katoucha ended her career as a model, after a long period in the wilderness. Two years later the star model was back in form again. But this time as a designer. She has worked hard on her designs and won many admirers, thanks to her collection 'Sublime barbarians', in which women are transformed by creations of raffia and silk. A nice nod in the direction of Africa and Europe. Now settled in London, Katoucha works, with great success, on her designer career.

Only a dozen names have found their way round the world. There are indeed very few black models to share a small slice of the cake - all that has been granted to them. They work in a niche market. It is not therefore surprising that we always see the same people in our magazines, on television and in video clips. But one tends to forget that there are hundreds who have been charmed by this uncertain, risky occupation. Often they do not get past the stage of doing fittings or small shows without any future. Without agents, they have only minor contracts or no contract at all. They are often obliged to do odd jobs as waitresses, hostesses or shop girls in order to make both ends meet. The most fortunate ones make a few appearances in advertisements. In catalogues. Others will have a role in a film. But they will all continue to dream of being queen of the catwalk, all their lives or just one night.

ELLE
GILLES BENSIMON

VOGUE
MATTHEW ROLSTON

ELLE
REGAN CAMERON

GIANNI VERSACE
MARIO TESTINO

PARIS MATCH
MARIO TESTINO

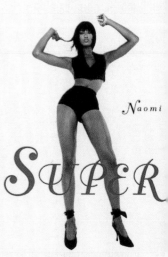

THE FACE
J.B. MONDINO

N° 337 - MAI 1998

AM NA
LE MAGAZINE DE LA FEMME

...NE PRINCESSE
AU SERVICE DES
AUTRES FEMMES

DONNEZ UNE CHANCE À LA LIBERTÉ

LE RETOUR DE TSHALA MWANA

NANE L. ANNAN
une épouse active

POUR LA BEAUTÉ DE VOS ONGLES

MAÎMOUNATA SIMPORÉ
Une sportive courageuse

INVITÉ DU MOIS
SAM MANGWANA

MAIRES
Mᵐᵉ BAYARD GAMATIE -
Mᵐᵉ M.A. HOUANGNI -
AMBOUROUE

MODE
SIMATEX - CICAM - AIMÉE BARY - MADE TONG -
DASHA - ESTERELLA- B.L. MODELS

M 1102 - 337 - 12,00 F

AMINA

LE MAGAZINE DE LA FEMME

NUMÉRO SPÉCIAL

MODE

AFRICAN
MOSAÏQUE
CLAIRE KANE
XARIT COUTURE
BINETA SALSAO
E. MARCEL
JOSÉ ESAM
A.D. COLLECTION

COIFFURE

BLACK TROPHY

LES KORA 97

CONCUBINAGE OU MARIAGE

LE FIMA AU NIGER

INVITÉ DU MOIS

MONGO BETI

Les affections cutanées spécifiques à la grossesse

Pays zone avion 1700 FCFA · Pays 28me surface 1200 FCFA · Belgique 145 FB · Suisse 6,3 FS · Canada 4,98 $ CAN · Guyane Antilles 20 F · Réunion 23 F · ISSN 0241-0338

Fashion in Africa, a personal view by Ethiopian top model Anna Getaneh

Page 176
Anna Getaneh on the cover of Amina
Courtesy of Amina, Paris France

Page 182
Masai dress shown in the African Mosaïque Show
© Ethiopian Children's Fund, Addis Ababa,
Ethiopia/New York, USA

African Mosaïque Show
© Ethiopian Children's Fund, Addis Ababa,
Ethiopia/New York, USA

Since the Ethiopian Children's Fund (E.C.F.) was founded in January 1993, we have attempted to build awareness, gain credibility and raise funds for the education and development projects, which we wanted to launch in Ethiopia. We are looking for an original concept, which could enable the foundation to exhibit a key facet of African culture, rather than focus on warfare and suffering, as so many others have done. E.C.F. wanted to display Africa's richness and diversity, its beauty, its hope for the future. Fashion was a natural move. African Mosaïque brings together traditional and contemporary African and Western designers who have drawn inspiration from Africa, on the same platform through the representation of cultural fashion shows. With my background as an international model from Ethiopia, and my experience as founder of African Mosaïque and the Ethiopian Children's Fund, I present my thoughts on fashion in Africa today.

Until recently, fashion was thought of as rather frivolous. Now, at last, it is being taken more seriously, talked about more than ever before. Fashion is 'in', and fashion designers and models are now often international celebrities. It is also acknowledged as a major industry (comparable in some countries to the motor or aviation industry), which gives work to millions of people around the world.

People suddenly appear to have realised that fashion is an aspect of culture – as of course it is! In fact, it is one of its most basic elements and, together with architecture and gastronomy, the one which comes closest to our everyday lives. Let us not forget that what fashion means is, quite simply, clothes – which were originally designed to protect us and keep us warm, and which now also serve as costume, as make-up, as expressions of the codes through which we reveal our selves, our social status, our true nature, even our day-to-day moods.

Fashion is a reflection of trends in society. Just as the influence of the West can be felt throughout the world, so Western fashion has spread to every continent. For men, jacket and trousers remain the universal classic costume, curiously unchanged for almost a century. More recently, at a less formal level, American-style jeans and T-shirts have conquered the world. For women, Western fashion is still seen by many as the acme of elegance. The Chanel suit (designed as long ago as 1954) and the Saint-Laurent 'smoking', to mention just two classic designs, are far from disapearring. Clearly, then, 'international' fashion is still essentially Western.

Some years ago, designers from Japan – Kenzo, Issey Miyake, Yohji Yamamoto and many others – burst joyfully onto this international scene and have now become an integral part of it. In the world of fashion, all influences are welcome. They are never rejected, for they encourage new design. Indeed, there is scarcely any field of culture in which such cross-fertilisation would not be beneficial. It looks as though this is the right moment to introduce something new for it seems that fashion design has temporarily run out of steam. There are various reasons for this. The moral crises of the fin-de-siècle? A general sense of gloom? A need to sit back and catch one's breath after the euphoric outburst of new design which has swept the world in recent years? There is undoubtedly another contributing factor – namely, the iron law of profit which has come to dominate the global economy, at the expense of the human dimension in business and at the

expense of design in the world of art. One after another, fashion houses are being bought up by increasingly powerful multinational concerns, all of which apply the same profit principle and thereby reduce the scope for design, which inevitably involves risk. Whatever the true causes may be, the recent rush of euphoria has now given way to a sense of weariness, of waiting, a demand for something new, and the attention is turning towards the new horizons.

What is Africa's role in all this? Africa is certainly present on the international scene, but African designers are few and far between. There is Tunisia's hugely talented Azzedine Alaïa, now considered one of the world's top designers, and Mali's Lamine Kouyaté, the darling of the fashion editors, whose label Xuly Bët continues to expand. But otherwise, sad to say, Africa is the least well represented of the world's continents. Yet Africa has so much to offer – as Parisian, American, Italian and Japanese designers know too well. At one time or another, they have all borrowed elements from this universal heritage and paid tribute to African aesthetics through their collections. Paco Rabanne, Yves Saint-Laurent, Kenzo, Romeo Gigli, Ralph Lauren, Donna Karan, Jean-Louis Scherrer, Thierry Mugler... the list is long.

Luckily, many African designers have become aware of the wealth of this heritage which, for all its universality, is above all their own. And the task of bringing it into the limelight and investigating its infinite potential is above all theirs. Yet African fashion is still in its infancy.

There is no shortage of talent in Africa, far from it. Indeed, why should Africans be any less talented in fashion than in other artistic fields in which they have gained international reputations? African musicians have established an unchallenged position on the international scene. Literally dozens of them are household names around the globe. In the visual arts, contemporary African artists are regularly exhibited in Europe, the United States and Japan. African fashion, on the other hand, still awaits a breakthrough. It has made great progress in design, but less so when it comes to organisation.

In major African cities, as elsewhere in the world, fashion shows in top hotels are broadcast on television, new fashion magazines are springing up everywhere girls dream of becoming fashion models. There is also a new, encouraging tendency to return to traditional clothing. In French-speaking Africa, the unexpected devaluation of the CFA franc has reinforced this trend. People have turned to traditional clothing, not just because it is cheaper than Western clothing, but also because it is a way of reasserting their African identity. Leading society ladies regularly wear traditional clothes on important occasions, and celebrities even see it as their duty to do so. In some parts of Africa, unfortunately, the impact of colonisation was so violent and authoritarian that traditional clothing has practically disappeared, together with local dialects. Africans' legitimate desire to rediscover their cultural roots will initially involve a period of research. Meanwhile, the West African boubou has replaced local traditional garments. Despite this clear tendency to return to traditional clothing, most widely available clothing is imported. Most of these imported clothing are not top of the line designs either. African designers are enjoying a recent wave of recognition, but mostly produce on a small scale – usually in their own workshops, helped by a network of local 'crafts' people, turning out quantities which are just enough to supply their own outlets and private customers. Most of them have no sponsors or production units in Africa. Ironically, traditional African textiles are often made in the Netherlands, Germany or Asia. There is also an unfortunate tendency to add synthetic components to them. On the other hand, silk has recently begun to be imported into Africa, allowing the creation of new fabrics which have enriched the local heritage.

The best-known fashion designers present their collections sporadically (whenever they are ready) at charity balls, where their shows are indeed no more than that, without any proper commercial underpinning. Most African designers are based in their home countries and supply local markets, but a small number are now making names for themselves internationally.

Senegal's highly talented Oumou Sy is one of the most encouraging examples, for she has attempted to introduce a greater degree of structure and commercial development. She is regularly asked to exhibit at major international fashion events and she already has sales outlets in various places around the world. Without in any way renouncing her African identity in her styling, she is gradually developing her own commercial approach in the world of international fashion.

Alphadi, who is the chairman of the Association of African Fashion Designers, is considered a real pioneer among African designers. In November 1998, in an effort to be one of the first to 'internationalise' his label, he will make a long-cherished dream come true by holding a major international fashion show FIMA in the Niger desert, attended by leading African and Western designers.

Algeria's Nassila and Morocco's Zineb Joundy divide their time between made-to-measure and ready-to-wear clothing, while Dora Milad, from Tunisia concentrates on made-to-measure designs. All three women are upholding North Africa's dressmaking traditions with great talent and passion.

Other African designers have chosen to set up business in Europe (Paris or London). Ly Dumas lives between Paris, where she owns a boutique and her native country, Cameroon, where she manufactures most of her clothing, and provides training for young designers. The Liberian designer Abraham has also settled in Paris, where he regularly presents his increasingly successful collections – which have caught our eye since the very earliest days of African Mosaïque. As for Katoucha, she is undoubtedly the most 'Parisian' of African designers. After a brilliant modelling career, she now designs her own collections, which are a perfect blend of African inspiration and Western taste. With a profound awareness of her African roots, she never misses an opportunity to support African fashion and takes part in every major event. South Africa's Linda Kulu, Cameroon's Made Jong, Zanzibar's Farouque Abdela and Magadascar's Eric Raisina are among an ever-increasing number of talented African designers whom we have had the pleasure working with.

So far we have only talked about clothing designers. Yet there is just as much talent in make-up, hairdressing, embroidery and all the other occupations that are connected with fashion. No, there is no shortage of talent in the African world of fashion. Various events (still too few in number) across the African continent have attempted to make this clear and, at the same time, provide a

Design by Paco Rabanne,
shown at the African Fashion Show,
FIMA, in Niger, 1998

Design by Xuly Bët, shown by top model Alek Wek
at the African Fashion Show, FIMA, Niger, 1998

commercial structure for designers and opportunities for them to meet. Such events include the Ktalezau fashion fair, the K'palezo fashion fair in Abidjan, the Sotiba textile show in Dakar, and the Caftan in Casablanca.

'This is an African moment... For the first time since Nancy Cunard rattled her tribal bangles and the exotic Josephine Baker was the sensation of Paris in the 1920s, African aesthetic of adornment seems right for modern fashion.', wrote the leading fashion journalist Suzy Menkes in the New York Times in April 1997. This is a special moment in the history of fashion, an opportunity to be seized by African designers. Never before has there been so much demand for what they have to offer. Every effort should now be made to help them. We know that the fashion industry generates wealth. It can provide an income for millions of Africans.

Of course, African fashion must continue to assert its identity in its designs, but it must also find its own ways of developing and of dealing with the international organisation of the fashion world. When the brilliant new generation of Japanese designers appeared some years ago, they brought not only their style but also their own ways of working. They became part of the international system without in any way renouncing their identity. When Azzedine Alaïa appeared on the international scene, he too established a position in his own way, using his own methods. Lamine Kouyaté's original, unconventional approach to fashion has likewise proved highly successful. Africans certainly have plenty to learn from the rigour and efficiency of Western methods. For too long, however, they were content simply to copy them, thereby missing out on the research which would have enabled them to discover, assert and develop their own methods and organisation.

The human dimension, which has too often been sacrificed in Western economic development, has always been a central feature of African society. The negociating process that precedes business deals may strike Europeans as a waste of time, but it is an essential aspect of social interaction between Africans. In Africa, personal commitment and respect for the other person's word matter more than a contract signed in duplicate.

Africa is a vast continent with many faces, a cultural mosaic whose pieces go to make up a unique, millennial whole. While contributing to the aesthetics of modern fashion, it must discover and develop its own way of working, its own organisation, without renouncing its true identity.

As we said it again and again: the talent is there. Now we need to encourage the right initiatives. Just as musicians need concerts and CDs to make their voices heard, fashion designers need fashion shows and magazines, of which there are still not enough in Africa. Designers need to meet and to compare what they are doing in competition with one another. They need to exhibit their work by every possible means. They need to show that the sources of African inspiration are more than just 'ethnic' or 'exotic'. Fashion is set to be one of the vehicles of African influence and economic development in tomorrow's world. The way now lies open for African fashion to assert itself on its own turf and to establish a position in the world of international fashion. It should be given all the help and support it needs to take advantage of this unique opportunity.

African Fashion Designers

Abraham Pelham

Adzedu of Shapes

Joël Andrianomearisoa

Alphadi

Katoucha

Martin Kapfumvuti

Mickaël Kra

Makeda

Oumou Sy

Xuly Bët

Abraham Pelham has developed a taste for beautiful fabrics and 'true chic'. After his studies at the University of Liberia he went to the United States to fulfil his dream of becoming a fashion designer. He attended classes at the Fashion Institute of Technology in New York and embarked on a successful American career. After taking part in the African Mosaïque fashion show, organised by the Ethiopean Children's Fund in Paris in 1996, he decided to settle in the French capital. In 1998 he designed his first couture line. For him, aesthetic perfection is the motor of his creativity.

Tetteh Adzedu graduated from the Ardis School of Fashion in Washington DC in 1978. He is the founder of the fashion house Adzedu of Shapes in Ghana and runs a school for fashion designers in Accra, the Adzedu African Fashion Institute. He is President of the Ghana Fashion Designers' Association and in 1990 he won a 'Ghana National Award for Export Achievement'. He says of himself that he is 'a militant for tradition'. Adzedu of Shapes is a frequent participant at fashion shows in Africa and the USA. He designs for the well-known Ghanaian singer Kojo Antwi and for several heads of state. Adzedu was awarded the Principal 1998 Prince Claus Award for preserving and reappraising African clothing tradition and adopting them to create contemporary fashion.

All designs by Adzedu of Shapes, Accra, Ghana
Photos: Eric-Don Arthur, Accra, Ghana

Tetteh Adzedu in his studio in Accra, Ghana
Photo: Eric-Don Arthur, Accra, Ghana

Joël Andrianomearisoa was only twelve when he enrolled at the fashion academy in his home city Antananarivo, where he was to win several first prizes. After completing his secondary education he went to classes at the Institut Métiers Arts Plastiques in Antananarivo in Madagascar. Since 1995 he experiments with different materials – wood, metal, stone and plastic. He presented his first fashion shows at the end of 1995, since when he has been producing new creations at a rapid rate. He frequently designs for stage and film productions in Madagascar and other countries, and is much in demand as a television scenery designer. In 1996 he won the Antananarivo 'Jeune Talent 96' trophy. Since September 1998 he has been attending classes in Architecture in Paris, France.

Design by Joël Andrianomearisoa, Antananarivo, Madagascar
© Revue Noire, Paris, France

Joël Andrianomerisoa, between his models wearing his designs
at a fashion show during the fashion week at Metissacana in Dakar,
Senegal, 1998
Photo: Jean-Claude Do Van
Courtesy Amina, Paris, France

Designs by Joël Andrianomearisoa, Antananarivo, Madagascar
© Revue Noire, Paris, France

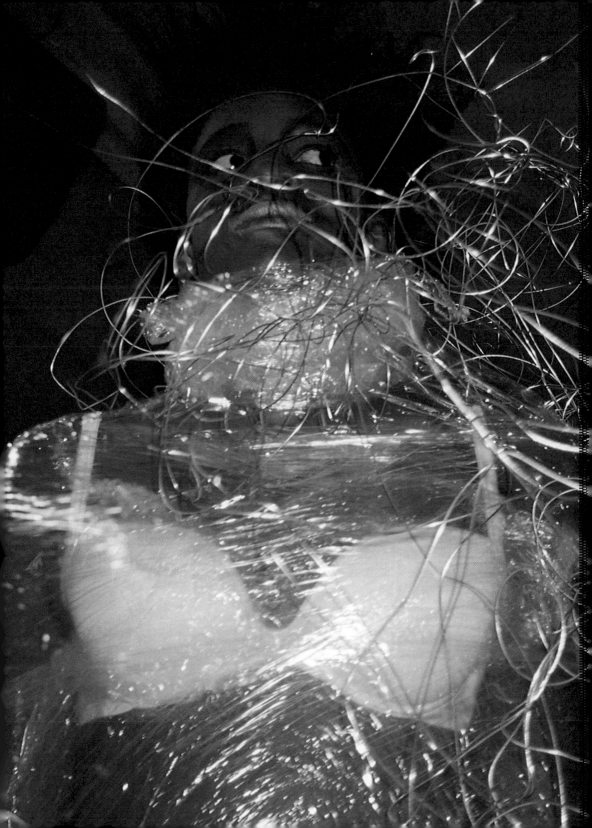

Alphadi is a graduate of the Chardon Savard Studio in Paris and the Fashion Institute of Technology in Washington DC. Together with other African designers he founded the Fédération Africaine des Créateurs and is the current President of the Association. He lives and works in Niamey, Niger. As 'a child of the desert' he seeks to maintain alive African traditions using traditional techniques in his creations, combining materials such as leather, silver and bronze with raw cotton, linen and silk. His creations are intended as a 'homage to the modern African woman'. In November 1998, Alphadi has organised the first 'Festival International de la Mode Africaine' (FIMA) in the desert of Niger. This event was orientated towards international exchanges in high fashion.

Alphadi was awarded the Principal 1998 Prince Claus Award for his high quality fashion and the promotion of an (international) fashion infrastructure for Africa.

Dress, design by Alphadi, Niamey, Niger
Photo: Alain Herman, Paris, France

Alphadi
Photo: Alain Herman, Paris, France

Design by Alphadi, Niamey, Niger shown
by top model Anna Getaneh at the FIMA Festival International
de la Mode Africaine in Niger, 1998

Design by Alphadi, Niamey, Niger
Photo: Alain Herman, Paris, France

Dress, design by Alphadi, Niamey, Niger
Photo: Alain Herman, Paris, France

Design by Alphadi, Niamey, Niger shown by
top model Alek Wek at the FIMA Festival International
de la Mode Africaine in Niger, 1998

Having spent most of her youth in Mali and Senegal, the twenty-year-old Katoucha went to Paris, where she soon made her name as a top model. She has worked with celebrated designers like Yves Saint-Laurent, Givenchy, Paco Rabanne and Azzedine Alaïa. She and Iman are the first African women to have launched a 'black attitude' in the world of fashion. After ending her modelling career she started her own design studio in 1996, where she has developed a style of her own. Faithful to her origins, she integrates Africa into her complete collection. Themes such as 'Out of Africa', 'Urban Caftan', 'Les Oiseaux', 'Les Parisiennes', 'African Rock' and 'Les Barbares Sublimes' play major roles in her work.

Indigo cotton dress 'debardeur',
design by Katoucha, London, UK
Photo Roberto Tecchio, Milan Italy
Courtesy of Katoucha

Raffia dress and jewellery design
'Sublime barbare' by Katoucha, London, UK
Photo Cecile Loudeur, Paris, France
Courtesy of Katoucha

Asymmetric top with trousers,
velvet and stainless steal,
design by Katoucha, London, UK
Photo Roberto Tecchio, Milan, Italy
Courtesy of Katoucha

Katoucha
Photo Christian Simon Pietri
Courtesy of Katoucha

Design by Katoucha, London, UK
at a fashion show in Abidjan, Ivory Coast, 1997
Photo and courtesy of Vlisco BV, Helmond,
the Netherlands

Design by Katoucha, London, UK
at a fashion show in Abidjan, Ivory Coast, 1997
Jewellery by Mickaël Kra, Abidjan,
Ivory Coast/Paris, France
Photo and courtesy of Vlisco BV, Helmond,
the Netherlands

Martin Kapfumvuti graduated in 1990 from the Bulawayo Poly-technic College, where he obtained the 'City and Guilds of London Institute Certificate in Hairdressing'. He won the Hairdressing Association of Bulawayo's 'Afro-Hair Free Styling Award' and the 'Revlon Southern African Competition'. Kapfumvuti, who has taken it upon himself to promote the hairdressing profession in Botswana, is secretary of the Health, Beauticians and Hairdressing Trade Advisory Committee. He advises hairdressers' schools and companies setting up new centres for trainee hairdressers. He has founded a national hairdressing training course where he tests the latest materials and techniques. He also runs a salon in which he organises workshops, demonstrations and internships.

Martin Kapfumvuti at work in his studio, Gaborone, Botswana/
all designs by Martin Kapfumvuti
Photos: Karin Duthie, Illustrative Options, Gaborone, Botswana

Mickaël Kra studied art history and interior design in Paris, subsequently obtaining a BA in Fine Arts at the Parsons School of Design in New York. In 1986 he designed a jewellery line called Reine Pokou. Inspired by hieroglyphs and geometrical forms used by the Ashanti in Ghana and the Ivory Coast, the collection is a contemporary adaptation of traditional ceremonial styles from old African kingdoms. Kra combines local craftsmanship, creativity, materials and cultural aspects of the Ivory Coast – where his roots lie – with the spirit of western commercial enterprise. After several years spent commuting between Abidjan, Paris and New York, Kra settled in Paris in 1993, where he launched a new, non-commercial label under his own name. He designs for a variety of top names in fashion, including Alphadi, Katoucha, Féraud, Yoko Ono and Balmain.

Jewellery design by Mickaël Kra,
Abidjan, Ivory Coast/Paris, France
Photo: Alain Herman, Paris, France
Courtesy of Mickaël Kra

Jewellery design by Mickaël Kra,
Abidjan, Ivory Coast/Paris, France
Photo: Alain Herman, Paris, France
Courtesy of Mickaël Kra

Jewellery design by Mickaël Kra,
Abidjan, Ivory Coast/Paris, France
Photo: Alain Herman, Paris, France
Courtesy of Mickaël Kra

Jewellery and dress design by Mickaël Kra,
Abidjan, Ivory Coast/Paris, France shown at the
FIMA Festival International de la Mode Africaine in Niger, 1998

Jewellery and dress design by Mickaël Kra,
Abidjan, Ivory Coast/Paris, France shown at the
FIMA Festival International de la Mode Africaine in Niger, 1998

Jewellery Absolut design by Mickaël Kra,
Abidjan, Ivory Coast/Paris, France
Photo: Service de presse, News Pepper, 1998

Aya Esther Konan was trained as a bookkeeper before switching to fashion. In 1987 she opened her own fashion house in Abidjan, where she was a successful participant in the designer contest 'Ciseaux d'Or'. She started designing her own jewellery line, Makeda, in 1992, inspired by traditional African art of the Akan and Ashanti peoples. In 1996 she set up Makeda Fusion, which markets her commercial designs. She currently presents three different lines. In November 1998 she participated in the FIMA, the African fashion show which was held in the desert of Niger.

Jewellery design by Makeda, Abidjan, Ivory Coast, 1998
Photo: Bruno de Medeiros, Abidjan, Ivory Coast

Family dressed in traditional cloths, jewellery design by Makeda, Abidjan, Ivory Coast, 1998
Photo: Bruno de Medeiros, Abidjan, Ivory Coast

Studio of Makeda, Abidjan, Ivory Coast, 1998
Photo: Bruno de Medeiros, Abidjan, Ivory Coast

Aya Konan
Photo: Bruno de Medeiros, Abidjan, Ivory Coast

Jewellery and dress design by Makeda, Abidjan, Ivory Coast shown at the FIMA Festival International de la Mode Africaine in Niger, 1998

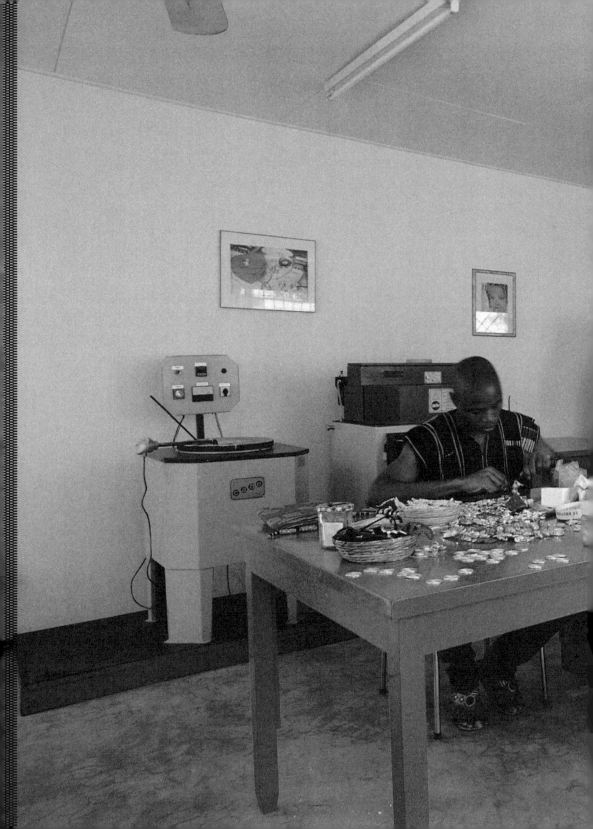

Oumou Sy is self-taught and lives and works in Dakar. She teaches at the Ecole des Beaux Arts and at the 'Ateliers de Stylisme et de Formation aux Arts et Techniques Traditionelles et Modernes du Costume et de la Parure en Afrique et en Occident', which she founded herself. Oumou Sy has designed costumes for African and foreign films and stage productions. In 1993 she won the prize for the best costumes at the Ouagadougou Film Festival, Burkina Faso, and the 'Professionali Cinema' prize in Milan. In 1995 she won another prize for the best costumes at the Johannesburg Film Festival. She founded the first Carnival of Dakar, in which participated 80 floats, 250 persons and 3 trucks, all decorated by Oumou Sy and the students of her school. Her theatrical collection 'Rois et Reines d'Afrique' mixes history with avant-garde and travels all over the globe. In November 1998, she participated in FIMA, an African fashion show in the desert of Niger. Oumou Sy was awarded the Principal 1998 Prince Claus Award for her major contribution to African fashion design and for her contribution to the setting up of a local, national and international infrastructure for African fashion.

Cyberdress, 1997, design by Oumou Sy, Dakar, Senegal
Photo: Mamadou Touré Béhan, Dakar, Senegal

Gold Woman, 1997, design by Oumou Sy, Dakar, Senegal
Photo: Mamadou Touré Béhan, Dakar, Senegal

Oumou Sy
Photo: Mamadou Touré Béhan, Dakar, Senegal

Design by Oumou Sy, Dakar, Senegal shown at the FIMA
Festival International de la Mode Africaine in Niger, 1998

Design by Oumou Sy, Dakar, Senegal shown at the FIMA
Festival International de la Mode Africaine in Niger, 1998

Designs by Oumou Sy at the Carnival, Dakar, Senegal
Photo: Mamadou Touré Béhan, Dakar, Senegal

Lamine Badian Kouyaté (Xuly Bët), studied architecture at the UPA University of Strasbourg, France, and at La Villette School of Architecture in Paris, France, before embarking on a career in fashion. In 1989 he launched the label Xuly Bët Funkin'Fashion Factory INC. – 'Xuly Bët' means 'wanna take my picture' in Wolof. In 1992 he presented his first spring/summer collection in black-and-white. A year later he featured in important New York fashion shows. Since then he has been associated with major labels such as 3 Suisses and Puma. Among his many awards are the 'Prix du ministère de la culture', the 'Vénus de la mode' and the 'Trophée de la mode 1996'. In 1998 he designed costumes for the inaugural ceremony at the 'Stade de France', and was invited to stage fashion shows in Argentina and Brazil. His clothes are found chiefly in small boutiques and in his own shops in Paris, New York and Marseilles.

XULY BËT

Design by Xuly Bët, Bamako, Mali/Paris, France
Photo: Gauthier Gallet, Paris, France
Courtesy Cristofoli Press

Design by Xuly Bët, Bamako, Mali/Paris, France
Photo: Gauthier Gallet, Paris, France
Courtesy Cristofoli Press

Design by Xuly Bët, Bamako, Mali/Paris, France
Photo: Gauthier Gallet, Paris, France
Courtesy Cristofoli Press

Design by Xuly Bët, Bamako, Mali/Paris, France
Photo: Gauthier Gallet, Paris, France
Courtesy Cristofoli Press

Designs 'Printemps-Eté' 1993,
by Xuly Bët, Bamako, Mali/Paris, France
Photo: Ammette Aviell, Paris, France
Courtesy Cristofoli Press

Design by Xuly Bët, Bamako, Mali/Paris, France
Photo: Gauthier Gallet, Paris, France
Courtesy Cristofoli Press

A

- Abacos = Mao-style suit with a cravat instead of a tie
- Kingdom of Abomey = was situated in the present-day Republic of Benin
- Adinkra fabric = Ashanti textile tradition of Ghana; Adinkra cloths are large pieces of cotton fabric stamped with motifs that have symbolic meanings. Worn primarily at funerals, adinkra cloth is also worn at some serious occasions (anniversary of the death; honour of a departed elder; during the mourning period, which can take up to a year). There are several kinds of adinkra cloths, each named according to its colour: dark russet (kuntunkuni), dark red (kobene), black (birisi). Today adinkra symbols are stamped on cloths of many bright colours. These cloths are worn on special occasions other than funerals as 'Sunday cloths', and adinkra symbols – the corpus comprises more than five hundred different motifs – are used to decorate stationery, jewellery, home and clothing design in North America.
- African Mosaïque = a collection of traditional African clothes and contemporary designs by designers from Africa and the West, which are shown to raise funds for the E.C.F., the Ethiopian Children's Fund
- Ambi = skin-lightening
- Antennes = wire-braiding
- Asante = the unbroken circle
- Ashanti = a people who populated Central Ghana, Kumasi region during the 17th century. The Ashantis (Asantes) are one section of the Akan people in Ghana. They are considered industrious, independent, handworking and ambitious.
- Aso oke pagne = ceremonial dress of the Yoruba people, Nigeria; worn at namings, betrothals, weddings, important birthdays, funerals and on Christian and Islamic holidays
- Austrian 'basin riche' = French and Wolof expression for heavy, expensive cotton damask made in Austria

B

- Bafana Bafana = the national soccer team of South Africa
- Bakhur = the burning of incense to perfume the body
- Bali bali bachi = special hair design of the 'sapeurs'. The sides of the head are completely shaved and the hair on top is cut very short giving the impression of a bold head. This style is inspired by the Congolese hair designs of the 1930s and 1950s.
- Bamana = a people living in Mali
- Bast fibre = botanical term describing vegetal tissues, linen woven from bast fibres
- Bamun = plangi technique with beaten bark from Cameroon
- Batik = method of decorating fabric used for centuries in Indonesia. With melted wax a design is applied to the cloth (cotton or silk), which is then dipped in cool, originally vegetable, dye. Areas covered by wax do not receive the dye and display a light pattern on the coloured ground. The process may be repeated several times. When the design is complete, the wax is removed in hot water. A crackling effect occurs if dye has seeped into cracks of hardened wax. The same or similar patterns have been used for about 1,000 years. Batik was brought to Europe by Dutch traders; the technique was adopted in the 19th century by western craftsmen, and is still widely used.
- Ibn Battuta = Arab traveller and geographer (born in Tanger in 1304 AD; died between 1368 and 1377). He visited the Sahara, Sudan and Niger. In 1355 he travelled to Tekrur, a kingdom in the middle of the valley of the river Senegal, populated by Toucouleurs. The Tekrur were a major economic force during the 11th and 12th centuries, before the emergence of the kingdom of Soso and the empire of Mali.
- Bindhi = a gem-like dot worn by married Indian women to signify a third eye or the acquisition of greater insight
- Bogolan = Malian 'mud cloth', a heavy cotton with geometric designs; result of a dyeing technique midway between batik and painting: mud-based dyes are used to paint outlines, as opposed to actual patterns, which remain colourless
- Boubou = West-African embroidered robes for men and women. A flowing, floor-length robe often embroidered at the neckline. Originally an Islamic dress adopted in the past two centuries
- Boul falé = 'stay cool' in Wolof
- Bozo = a people living in eastern Mali
- Brocade = weaving technique; term used for describing the effect of a design formed by a weave thread whose use is limited by the width of the motifs

C

- Caftan = Moroccan long dress with long sleeves
- Chadari = head-to-toe covering for women, with lacework covering the eyes, worn in Iran and Afghanistan
- Chèche = head-covering worn by Tuareg men. Is usually made of black or white cloth (black for work and white for public occasions) and may be anything from six to ten metres in length. Its length may even be the subject of a contest to see who can wear the longest piece of cloth without the whole thing falling apart! The chèche has undergone several variations in response to fashion: from the classic colours black and white, it briefly shifted to blue, and for a while a raw shade of yellow was for sale in Tamanrasset (Algeria).

- CFA = the currency of a large area of francophone Africa; 1 USD = 555 CFA (November 1998); 1 FF = 100 CFA
- Coiffe = headdress; from a misread sign on the window of a Congolese hairdresser in Paris
- Coura Thiaw = a Wolof dancer who was very famous in the thirties, especially in Saint-Louis, the former capital of Senegal
- Cowry = a small shell used for coin in parts of Africa

D

- Dida = plangi technique with raffia from Ivory Coast
- Dirriankhe = slang term for elegant, corpulent women, associated with contemporary, wealthy women traders (in use in Senegal)
- Disquettes et grotos = slang expression in Senegal and Ivory Coast, meaning sugar daddy, referring to relationships between young female students and older men, a phenomenon of urban Ivorian life
- Djellaba = a long hooded tunic, worn in the Maghreb
- Dogon = an animist people that fled to the remote cliffs of eastern Mali in the 14th and 15th centuries to escape conversion by invading Fulani Muslims from the South
- Dukhan = vapour-bath
- Dutch wax = fabric made with batik technique originally from Indonesia, appropriated and industrialised by the Dutch. The Dutch wax is made in Helmond by Vlisco BV and is distributed in Africa.

F

- Faso dan fani = traditional cotton fabric now woven at a factory in Ouagadougou, Burkina Faso, from locally grown cotton
- Fuug jaay = disdained second-hand clothing, commercialised in Africa
- Fuug jaay tailor = tailor who transforms second-hand clothes into fashionable outfits

G

- Génito = an impoverished male university student who pursues wealthy older women
- Ghazal = Arabic love poetry
- Griot = story-teller
- Guinée = a length of indigo produced in the French Indian colony of Pondicherry

H

- Haalpulaar = Toucouleur = one of the major ethnic groups in Senegal
- Haïk = thick fabric used for making veils; outer garment made of a long piece of woollen material, covering the body and the head

- Hambel = North African Berber blanket, decorated with geometric symbols such as crosses, triangles and vertical bars. They are usually used in interiors as floor covers, room dividers, or bedding. In the early 16th century, they were traded by the Portuguese all over the West African coast to obtain slaves and gold. Peggy Stoltz Gilfoy assesses that the wool fragments – dated from the 11th to the 18th century – found in burial caves in Mali were a local attempt to copy the North African imported hambels.
- Hannana = woman who practises henna art professionally
- Herero = a people living in Namibia. Their traditional dress was in German style, imposed by the missionaries, as worn by German settlers in South Africa around 1800

I

- Id-ul-Hajj = Muslim feast at the end of the period of the annual pilgrimage to Mecca, celebrated throughout the Islamic world and the main occasion for exchanging gifts
- Ikat = technique, in which the warp threads are dyed before the weaving process

J

- Jacarde = a light-weight synthetic fabric. The type marketed in Saudi Arabia and sold in Senegal is said to be made in Japan or Taiwan (cheaper quality). Like damask, it has an inwoven motif (flowers, leaves) in the same colour thread to produce the effect of a relief
- Java = fabric made by Vlisco BV in the wax technique (see Dutch wax) with an Indonesian inspired design
- Jebba = traditional long tunic for men and women in Tunisia
- Jelwa = unveiling of the bride (North Africa)

K

- Kaasa or Khasa = woollen blanket of the Peul, Mali, produced on the double-heddle loom by the Fulani Maabube weavers
- Kabba = ceremonial costume worn by the nobility and orthodox clergymen in Ethiopia
- Kali = a devouring, destructive goddess in Hinduism. Kali is often represented with her four hands variously holding a sword, a shield, the severed hand of a giant, or a strangling noose, or else stretched out in a gesture of assurance.
- Kanaga patterns = patterns on masks of the Bamana people, Mali
- Kao kao = new residents of Dakar
- Kente = cottons or silks, hand-woven by Ashanti communities, based on blue and yellows, for formal wear. Also known as Asasia cloth.
- Khartoum = low-cost, sheer cotton produced in East Asia and used for ndockettes and wraparound style clothes

- el-Kiswa el-kbira= the 'great covering', bridal dress in Tunisia
- Kita = dyed wrap from Ghana, Mali, Nigeria
- Kitambala = neckerchief
- Kohl= finely powdered galena in a shade of dark blue; applied around the eyes. It possesses the magic virtue of making the eyes seem larger. It is applied to the eyelids of newborn infants before first exposing them to the sun.
- K'palezo = international event for African fashion creators in Abidjan, Ivory Coast
- Kuba = plangi technique with raffia from Ivory Coast
- Kwanzaa = annual festival for African Americans in the USA
  L
- Lancé = French for effect of design shaped by a weave thread which runs through the entire width of the tissue, but which has no part in the formation of the effects of the background. The weave threads do not appear on the surface of the tissue unless for additional effects of the designs the tissue produces.
- Lawsonia inermis = 'henna-plant'; small shrub found in Africa
- Laylat al-hinna = 'the night of the henna'; the night before the wedding, during which henna is applied
- Libaya = a top
- Patrice Lumumba = (1925-1961), first prime minister of the Congo (now the Democratic Republic of the Congo). He became president of the multi-ethnic National Congolese Movement; when the Congo attained independence in 1960, he became prime minister. Lumumba was dismissed by President Joseph Kasavubu and later assassinated. He was proclaimed a national hero and martyr in 1966.
  M
- Malinké = language of the Wanaga people
- Mami Wata = patron of the sea for the coastal people of Nigeria and Sierra-Leone (Mami = mother; Wata = derived from water). She appears as a fair-skinned woman with very long hair, surrounded by snakes or as a siren.
- Mande = comprises several ethnic groups living in the Sudan-Sahel zone of Eastern Africa. Originally from the empires of Ghana and Mali
- Mandjak = a people living in the South of Senegal (Casamance) and in Guinea Bissau
- Marabout = Islamic religious leader in Muslim Africa (member of a West African brotherhood) believed to possess supernatural powers; syncretic healer using traditional medicines and amulets
- Masai = people living in Kenya and Tanzania; cattle farmers, famous for their tallness and beautiful jewellery

- Mbubb = Wolof word for boubou
- Melia = garment worn by Bedouin women in Tunisia, in a wide range of colours
- Modou modou = transnational Mouride
- al-Mokhala = the vial of kohl
- Moucharaby = projecting ariel window with a wooden latticework shutter
- Mouride = member of the Mouride Muslim brotherhood, commercially active in the informal sector and expanding its networks in the Diaspora throughout the world
- Mouridism = major current of Islam in Senegal; an Islamic brotherhood (Sufi order)
  N
- Ndebele = people living in South-Africa, famous for their beadwork and geometric paintings on the walls of their homes
- Ndockette = Euro-African style dress with wide sleeves from the Senegalese coastal trading zones. Now popular throughout the region. It is also the main export item sold to traders in Dakar markets, in Jeddah, New York and Paris.
- Négritude = ideology at the beginning of this century that idealised black roots, and revalued African identity
- Nocci = openwork embroidery
- Nuba = a people living in western Sudan, in the South-east of the province of Kordofan
  P
- Pagne = cotton fabric worn as a (wrap)skirt or a shawl for men and women; width 120 cm, length varies from 2-12 yards
- Paki dot = derisory for a bindhi
- Peul = a nomadic people living throughout the sub-Saharan region; part of the Pulaar language group
- Plangi = tie-and-dye technique; one or more threads are used to tie off parts of the fabric very tightly. This prevents the dye from penetrating all the way through. Small pebbles, shells, cotton or indigo seeds may also be inserted. After the fabric has been dyed and dried, the tied-off parts are untied and patterns of circles, dots, discs, rings or diamonds appear.
- Pulaar = language (and ethnic group) throughout West Africa; main language in Senegal
  Q
- Qasida = Arabic epic poetry
  R
- Radio aerials = wire-braiding
  S
- SAFDA = South African Fashion Designers Association, based in Johannesburg and providing a platform for black designers in South Africa

- Safsari = wrap worn by Tunisian women
- Safsari hrir = a rectangle of ivory-coloured silk (4.40 metres long and 1.45 metres wide) which is woven on a hand-loom in Tunis. Alternating strips of dull and shiny fabric, woven lengthways give it its unusual appearance.
- Sanse = Wolof word for fancy dress
- SAPE = 'Société des Ambianceurs et Personnes Elégantes': Society of Makers of Atmosphere and Elegant People
- Sapeur = member of SAPE
- Saree = traditional Indian wrapcloth for women
- Senegambia = total of Senegal and Gambia
- Shamma = Ethiopian cotton shawl worn by men and women
- Shammane = trained weavers in Ethiopia
- Shawal baz = Pakistani dress
- SIAO = the international handicrafts fair in Ouagadougou, Burkina Faso
- Signares = slave traders' companions
- Soninké = language of the Wanaga people
- Sotiba = 'Société de Textile': textile industry association in Senegal
- Suki yamaboko = braid
  T
- Tabaski = commemoration of Abraham's sacrifice, celebrated in Islam
- Tapp = Wolof word for a special press technique of textile
- Tchatcho colours = slang term for skinlightner, which turns the skin orange like a papaya
- Tibeb = multi-coloured patterned band of silk or rayon on a shamma, an Ethiopian cotton shawl worn by men and women
- Toucouleur = Haalpulaar = ethnic group living throughout West-Africa; major ethnic group in Senegal
- Taille basse = European style dress from the West-African coastal trading zones
- Touba = Holy city of the Mouride Muslim brotherhood; often used in names of enterprises and homes
- Tritik = stich and dye technique in which three-dimensional areas are isolated by pleating, gathering or rolling so that the dye cannot penetrate. The stitching is done either by hand or by machine. Parts of the fabric may be isolated by means of embroidery
- Tubaab = Wolof word for foreigner
- Tuub = Wolof word for hand-dyed cloth
  W
- Walo walo = lit. 'braids' = Wolof ethnic group
- Wolof = one of the main ethnic groups in Senegal, holds language and cultural hegemony in the coastal and urban areas, and also nationally

- Woodin = label of contemporary fabrics and designs. Woodin is a sister company of Vlisco BV in Helmond, the Netherlands
  X
- Xessal = skin-lightening
- Xew = Wolof word for family ceremonies
- Xhosa = major ethnic group in the Cape area of South Africa. Xhosa dress is considered traditional nowadays. It resembles the long skirt and apron worn by the wives of European settlers.
  Z
- Zar = ritual and tradition related to spirit possession. It is widely practised among women in the Sudan, Ethiopia and the southern part of Egypt. During the ceremony of Zar women sing and dance and go into trance-like state, impersonating several characters (even male characters). Such impersonation is a vehicle for expressing wishes and seeking desires, which under normal circumstances may not be fulfilled. In the analyses of many scholars, Zar is considered a source of empowerment for women in such societies.
- Zazou = soda-based hair-straightener
- Zerzhana = jebba worn inside-out as a sign of mourning (Tunisia)

- *Aditi, The Living Arts of India*, Smithsonian Institution Press, Washington DC, 1989
- Al-Bakri; *Géographe andalou*, in: Cuocq, J.; Recueil des sources arabes concernant l'Afrique occidentale du VIIIe au XVIe siècle, CNRS, Paris, 1975
- *Amina*, Magazine for Women in Africa, Paris, France, all issues 1998
- Aubaille-Sallenave, F.; *Les voyages de henné*, in: Journal d'Agriculture traditionelle et de botanique appliquée, April-June 1982
- Barry, Boubacar; *Commerce et commercants sengeambiens dans la longue duree: étude d'une formation economique dependante*, in: Commerce et commercants en Afrique de l'Ouest: Le Sénégal, l'Harmattan, Paris, 1992
- Bernezat, Odette; *Hommes des montagnes du Hoggar*, Editions des 4 seigneurs, Grenoble, 1975
- Biaya, T. K.; *Mundele, ndumba et ambiance. Le vrai bal blanc et noir. Aux sources de la sociabilité urbaine zaïroise*, in: G. de Villers (ed.), Belgique/Zaïre: quel avenir? Actes du colloque, Cahiers africains, 1994
- Biaya, T.K.; *Les paradoxes de la masculinité africaine moderne: une histoire de violences, d'immigration et de crises*, in: Canadian Folklore, 19,1: 99-112, 1997
- Boddy, Janice Patricia; *Wombs and Alien Spirits, Women, Men, and the Zar Cult in Northern Sudan*, University of Wisconsin Press, Madison, Wisconsin, 1989
- Bolland R.; *Tellem Textiles, Archaeological Finds from Burial Caves in Mali's Bandiagara Cliff*, Royal Tropical Institute, Amsterdam, 1991
- Boone, Catherine; *Merchant Capital and the Roots of State Power in Senegal, 1930-1985*, Cambridge University Press, Cambridge, 1992
- Boone, Sylvia; *Radiance From the Waters: Ideals of Feminine Beauty in Mende Art*, New Haven, Yale University Press, 1986
- Boulègue J.; *Le grand Jolof (XIII-XVIe siècles)*, Editions Façades, 1987
- Cohen, Rona I.; *A Jewish Yemenite Henna Ceremony and its Dances*, in: Journal of the Association of Graduate Dance Ethnologists, Spring 1981, Vol. 5
- Coquet M.; *Textiles africains*, Editions Adam Biro, Paris, 1995
- Diop, C. A.; *Antériorité des civilisations nègres: mythe ou vérité historique?*, Présence africaine, Paris, 1967
- Diop, Abdoulaye Bara; *La famille wolof: tradition et changement*, karthala., Paris, 1985
- Diop, Momar Coumba (ed.); *Essays in Statecraft*, Codesria, Dakar, Senegal, 1993
- Diouf, Mamadou; *Urban Youth and Senegalese Politics*: Dakar, 1988- 1994 in: Public Culture 8, 1996
- Ebin, Victoria; *The Body Decorated*, Thames and Hudson, New York, 1979
- Evans, N.; *Everything You Need to Know About Hairlocking, Dread, African & Nubian Locks*, A & B Publishers Group, Brooklyn, New York, 1996
- Fabius, Carine; *Mehndi, the Art of Henna Body Painting*, Three Rivers Press, New York, 1998
- Fall, Sokhna; *Seduire: cinq leçons senagalaises*, Editions Alternatives, Paris, 1998
- Fanon, Frantz; *Black Skin, White Mask*, Pluto Press, London, UK, 1986
- Faris, James; *Nuba Personal Art*, Duckworth, London, 1972
- Fatou Niang Siga Niang; *Reflets de traditions et modes saint-louisiennes*, Editions Khoudjia, Saint Louis, Senegal, 1989
- *On Transvesticism in Yoruba Society*, in: Fashion Theory, a Journal from Berg Press, UK
- Fauque, Claude and Otto Wollenweber; *Tissus d'Afrique*, Syros alternatives, Paris, 1991
- Fernandes V.; *Description de la côte occidentale d'Afrique (Sénégal, Cap de Monte, Archipels) (1506-1507)*, Centro de Estudos de Guiné Português, Bissau, 1951. French translation by T. Monod, A. Texeira da Mota and R. Mauny
- Fernandes V.; *Description de la côte occidentale d'Afrique de Ceuta au Sénégal, (1506-1508)*, Larose, Paris, 1938. French translation by P. de Cenival and T. Monod
- Gandoulou, Justin-Daniel; *Dandies à Bacongo: Le culte de l'élégance dans la société congolaise contemporaine*, l'Harmattan, Paris, 1989 and Karthala, Paris, 1994
- Gilfoy Stoltz, Peggy; *Patterns of Life, West African Strip-weaving Traditions*, Smithsonian Institution, Washington DC, 1986
- Gorfain, Phyllis, Deborah Kapchan and Katherine Young; *Wedding Song: Henna Art among Pakistani Women in New York City*, in: Journal of American Folklore, winter 1996, Vol. 109, no. 143
- Hansen, Karen; *Dealing with Used Clothing: Saluala and the Construction of Identity in Zambia's Third Republic*, in: Public Culture 6, 1994
- Hassan, Salah and Okwui Enwezor; *New Visions, Six Contemporary African Artists*, Zora Neale Hurston Museum of Art, Florida, 1994

- Hassan, Salah; *Genders and Nations*, Herbert F. Johnson Museum of Art, Ithaca, 1998
- *Henna (Mehndi), Body Art Handbook, Complete How-To Guide*, Phoenix & Arabeth, 1997
- Henriques, F.; *Family and Colour in Jamaica*, Secker & Warburg, London, 1953
- Hinna', *Encyclopédie de l'Islam, Nouvelle Edition*, E.J. Brill, Leiden/ Maisone Neuve et Larose, Paris, 1971
- hooks, bell; *Black Looks, Race and Representation*, South End Press, Boston, Massachusetts, 1992
- *HRAFlex Books*, MW1-001 Ethnography Series, 1984
- Jereb, James F.; *Arts and Crafts of Morocco*, Chronicle Books, San Francisco, 1995
- Jewsiewicki, B.; *De l'art africain et de l'esthétique, valeur d'usage, valeur d'échange*, in: Cahiers d'études africaines, 141-142, XXXVI, 1-2: 257-269, 1996
- Kanafani, Aida Sami; *Aesthetics and Ritual in the United Arab Emirates*, The American University of Beirut, 1983
- La société wolof: *Tradition et changement: les systèmes d'inégalité et de domination*, Karthala, Paris, 1981
- *Les costumes traditionnels féminins de Tunisie*, Collectif, Maison tunisienne de l'édition, Tunis, 1978
- Matory, James Roland; *Sex and the Empire that is no More*: University of Minnesota Press, Minneapolis, 1992
- Mauny, R., *Décorations des mains au henné*, in: Bulletin de l'IFAN, TXII, nr. 3, July, 1950
- Manniche, Lise; *An Ancient Egyptian Herbal*, British Museum Publications, Ltd., London, 1989
- Mercer, K.; *Welcome to the Jungle*, New Positions in Cultural Studies, Routledge, New York, London, 1994
- Messina, Maria; *Henna Party: An Orange-red Cosmetic Raises Moroccan Women's Spirits*, in: Natural History, 1988, Vol. 97 (9)
- Mustafa, Hudita Nura; *Practising Beauty: Crises, Value and the Challenge of Self-Mastery in Dakar, 1970- 1994*, Ph.D. dissertation, Harvard University, 1998
- Pérez, Annie (ed.); *Touches d'exotisme, XIVe – XXe siècles*; Musée de la mode et du textile, union centrale des arts décoratifs, Paris, France
- *Recensement nationale de l'artisanat*, Ministère de l'Industrie, du Commerce et de l'Artisanat, Dakar, Senegal, 1992
- Renne, Elisha; *The Cloth that Does not Die: The Meaning of Cloth in Bunu Social Life*, University of Washington Press, Seattle, 1993
- *Revue Noire*, special issue on fashion, December 1997-January/February 1998
- Roberts, N. P. and A.F. Roberts (eds.); *Memory, Luba Art and the Making of History*, Prestel – Museum for African Art, Munich/New York, 1996
- Roome, Loretta; *Mehndi: The Timeless Art of Henna Painting*, St. Martin's Griffin, New York, 1998
- Rose, T.; *Black Noise Rap Music and Black Culture in Contemporary America*, Wesleyan University Press, Hanover & London, 1994
- Rubin, Arnold (ed.); *Marks of Civilization, Artistic Transformations of the Human Body*, Museum of Cultural History, University of California, Los Angeles, 1988
- Sagay, E.; *African Hair Style*, Heinemann, London, 1983
- Said, Edward W.; *Orientalism*, Pantheon Press, New York, 1978
- Saksena, Jogendra; *Art of Rajasthan: Henna and Floor Decorations*, Sundeep, Delhi, India, 1979
- Schneider, Jane and Annette Weiner (eds.); *Cloth and Human Experience*, Smithsonian Institution Press, Washington, 1991
- Searight, Susan; *The Use and Function of Tattooing on Moroccan Women*, New Haven, USA
- Slyomovics, Susan and Amanda Dargan (Directors); *Wedding Song: Henna Art among Pakistani Women in New York City*, Video, 1990
- Sow, Fatou; *Femmes et valeurs africaines*, in: Bulletin d'IFAN, 19, 3, 1985
- Sylla, Assane; *La philosophie morale des Wolof*, Sankore, Dakar, Sengegal, 1978
- Tauzin, Aline; *Le henné, art des femmes de Mauritanie*, Ibis Press, 1998, Paris, France
- Tauzin, A., *Des couleurs et des voiles, practique de la teinture chez les Maures à Nouakchott (Mauritanie), littérature orale arabo-berbère, 16-17, 1985-86*, in: Al Wasit, 2, 1998
- Torgovnick, Mariana; *Gone Primitive*, University of Chicago Press, Chicago, 1990
- Vonderheyden, M., *Le henné chez les Musulmans de l'Afrique du Nord*, in: Journal des sociétés des Africanistes, t IV, 1934
- Westermarck, E., *Les cérémonies du mariages au Maroc*, Editions Ernest Leroux, Paris, 1921
- Westermarck, E., *Ritual and Belief in Morocco*, Mac Millan and Co., London, 1926

TSHIKALA K. BIAYA

Tshikala K. Biaya (1950, Democratic Republic of Congo) is an Associate Researcher at the Council for the Development of Social Science Research in Africa (Codesria), Dakar, Senegal. He is the author of numerous publications and articles on gender, religions, popular arts and cultural change in urban Africa. He is now preparing publications about 'Conflict in West-Africa' and 'Dance and its Dynamic Interaction in African and Diaspora Popular Culture'. Biaya is the co-ordinator of 'Conflict Prevention in West Africa', a joint project of the Netherlands Institute of International Relations, Clingendael, and Codesria, Senegal, and lectures at several universities in Africa, the USA and Canada.

ANNA GETANEH

Anna Getaneh (Ethiopean) is an Ethiopian top model. While pursuing her career as an international model, she has for some years chaired and helped to organise the Ethiopian Children's Fund (E.C.F.), based in New York and Addis Ababa. The Ethiopian Children's Fund supports in several ways (medicines, food supply, education) African children who suffer the effects of warfare, malnutrition and despair. In collaboration with Pharmaciens Sans Frontières, the E.C.F. is constructing a village in Ethiopia where children can find the necessary support, comfort and education needed for building their future.

SALAH M. HASSAN

Salah Hassan (Sudan) is an Assistant Professor of African and African Diaspora, Art History and Visual Culture at Africana Studies and Research Center, Cornell University, Ithaca, USA. He published and edited several books in the field of the arts and served as a guest curator for several exhibitions. He is editor of 'NKA Journal of Contemporary African Art', and serves as consulting editor for the magazine 'African Arts' and 'Atlantica International Journal of Contemporary Art'. Hassan is interested in human rights and democratisation issues in Africa and has been a member of the Sudan Human Rights Organisation since its revival in London in 1989.

MOUNIRA KHEMIR

Mounira Khemir (1959, Tunisia) is a free-lance curator of art exhibitions and former researcher at the Institut du Monde Arabe in Paris. She regularly lectures on the history of photography and on the importance of the image and aesthetics in representation in the Arab world. Khemir is the author of numerous articles and publications concerning photography, amongst which 'L'Orientalsime, L'Orient des photographes au XIXieme siècle' (1994) and 'Retrats de l'anima, fotografia africana' (1997).

MARIE-AMY MBOW

Marie-Amy Mbow (1960, Senegal) is an archaeologist and textile researcher at the Institut Fondamental d'Afrique Noire, University of Cheikh Anta Diop, Dakar, Senegal. Next to her research activities she is an expert on textile and a curator at the Musée d'Art Africain in Dakar, Senegal. She is in charge of several projects of the museum. Mbow is the author of numerous publications and articles on the subject of archaeology and culture, amongst which 'Gestion des ressources côtières et littorales du Sénégal' (1993) and 'Les musées: des attractions touristiques?' (1998).

RENÉE MENDY

Renée Mendy (1970, Senegal) is a journalist for 'Amina', an African magazine concerning women's issues, fashion and culture and the editor in chief of 'La Route', a magazine focusing on different cultures in order to inform travellers. Mendy has been a deputy editor in chief for the magazine 'Black Men'; she has been working as a co-host at 'MCM Africa Club', and as a reporter and an editor for Radio International France.

HUDITA NURA MUSTAFA

Hudita Nura Mustafa (1964, United Kingdom) is a researcher at the Human Sciences Research Council, Pretoria, South Africa. She has been a lecturer at several American universities and is the author of several publications and articles concerning the cultural importance of fashion in constructing identity and as an economical force. Mustafa wrote her dissertation on 'Practicing Beauty: Crises, Value, and the Challenge of Self-Mastery in Dakar, 1970-1994'. At present several articles are under review, amongst, which 'The State of Fashion: Popular Processes and Official Initiatives' and 'Portraits of Modernity: Fashioning Selves in Dakar'.

ELS VAN DER PLAS

Els van der Plas (1960, the Netherlands), Director of the Prince Claus Fund, is an art historian, art critic and curator. She is the founder and former Director of the Gate Foundation in Amsterdam (1988-1997), an organisation for intercultural exchange in the field of contemporary art. She has lectured at various Universities in the Netherlands and abroad and has contributed to many catalogues and art magazines, such as 'Art and Asia Pacific' and 'Third Text'.

AMINATA DRAMANE TRAORÉ

Aminata Dramane Traoré (Mali) has been the Minister of Culture and Tourism of the Republic of Mali since 1997. She is a cultural promoter and has founded and been active in various NGOs in the field of culture and development in Africa. She has published numerous reports, articles and books in this field, such as 'Autour de la danse indansable' (1998) and 'Mains des femmes' (1996), her autobiography.

MARLOUS WILLEMSEN

Marlous Willemsen (1969, the Netherlands), Policy Officer for the Prince Claus Fund, studied Arabic Language and Culture at Utrecht University, the Netherlands, and Islamic Art at Otto Friedrich University in Bamberg, Germany. Before joining the Prince Claus Fund she managed the Centre of Islamic Culture in Rotterdam (1994-1997), which runs partnerships with cultural organisations in the Middle East and North Africa.

Maison Alaïa, Paris, France

Phillipe Angelotti, Paris, France

Alexis B.A. Andandé, Director of the West African Museums Programme, Dakar, Senegal

Michel de Breteuil, Amina, Paris, France

Bernard Césari, IBIS Press, Paris, France

Josiane Christofoli, Christofoli Presse, Paris, France

Nini van Driel, Amsterdam, the Netherlands

Jean-Louis Dumas, Ethiopian Children's Fund, Paris, France

Fred Ernst, Reuters, Amsterdam, the Netherlands

Michel Mavros, Metissacana, Dakar, Senegal

Achille Mbembe, Codesria, Dakar, Senegal

Sonwabile Ndamasa, South African Designers Association, Johannesburg, South Africa

Hervé Panna, bureau Alphadi, Paris, France

Jean Pierre Tagornet, Al-Quobba Zarqua, Casablanca, Morocco

Mart Visser, fashion designer, Amsterdam, the Netherlands

Ton de Wit, Amsterdam, the Netherlands/Cascas, Senegal

Sue-an van der Zijpp, Groninger Museum, Groningen, the Netherlands

WITH SPECIAL THANKS TO

Vlisco BV, Helmond, the Netherlands

AND WITH THANKS TO

Amina, Paris, France

Elite, Amsterdam, the Netherlands

House of Orange, Amsterdam, the Netherlands

Messina Productions, Amsterdam, the Netherlands

Name Models, Amsterdam, the Netherlands

Theatex, Vinkenveen, the Netherlands

COLOPHON

The Art of African Fashion is published to mark the presentation of the Principal 1998 Prince Claus Award
to The Art of African Fashion. The award has been presented to Alphadi (Niger), Oumou Sy (Senegal) and
Tetteh Adzedu (Ghana). The publication also accompanies the exhibition 'African Fashion Design'
in the Stedelijk Museum Amsterdam from 12 December 1998 until 31 January 1999.

Published by: Prince Claus Fund, The Hague, the Netherlands/
Africa World Press, Asmara, Eritrea/New Jersey, USA
Editors: Prince Claus Fund, Els van der Plas, Marlous Willemsen
Photographers: Karin Duthie, Gaborone, Botswana; Mamadou Touré Béhan, Dakar, Senegal;
Bruno de Medeiros, Abidjan, Ivory Coast; Alain Herman, Paris, France; Eric Don-Arthur, Accra, Ghana
Production: Prince Claus Fund, Jeannette Kruseman, Carla Wauman
English-language editor: Tony Parr, Maastricht; Ruth Koenig, Buren ('Glossary'/'cvs')
Translators French-English: Kevin Cook, Nijmegen; Hazel Wachters, Pijnacker ('Models!')
Design: Irma Boom, Amsterdam
Printing: Drukkerij Rosbeek, Nuth

Prince Claus Fund
Hoge Nieuwstraat 30
2514 EL The Hague, Netherlands
Telephone: +31.70.427.4303
Telefax: +31.70.427.4277
E-mail: prclausf@wxs.nl
Website: www.princeclausfund.nl

Afrcia World Press, Inc.
P.O Box 1892   – P.O. Box 48
Trenton, NJ 08607   – Asmara, Eritrea
Telephone: +1. 609.844.9583
Telefax: +1.609.844.0198
E-mail: awprsp@africanworld.com
Website: www.africanworld.com

ISBN 0-86543-726-2 [English Edition]

Africa World Press, Inc.

P.O. Box 1892
Trenton, NJ 08607

P.O. Box 48
Asmara, ERITREA

C
Fonds

Dress, design by
Azzedine Alaïa,
Paris, France